M000035523

A *Guide to*
GENEALOGICAL RESOURCES
in Cincinnati and Hamilton County, Ohio

8ʰ Edition

Connie Stunkel Christman & Kenny R. Burck

Hamilton County Genealogical Society

A Guide to
GENEALOGICAL RESOURCES
in Cincinnati and Hamilton County, Ohio

8ʰ Edition

Connie Stunkel Christman & Kenny R. Burck

Hamilton County Genealogical Society

Cincinnati, Ohio
2019

Published by the
Hamilton County Genealogical Society
P.O. Box 15865
Cincinnati, OH 45215-0865
513-956-7078
https://hcgsohio.org

Cover illustration of "Die Hängebrücke über den Ohio," the Cincinnati Suspension Bridge; Max Burgheim, *Cincinnati in Wort und Bild* (M. & R. Burgheim: Cincinnati, 1888), 225.

Copyright 2019, Hamilton County Genealogical Society. All rights reserved. No part of this book may be reproduced or transmitted in any form or by any means, electronic or mechanical, including photocopying, recording or by any information storage and retrieval system without permission from the chapter, except for the inclusion of brief quotations in a review.

Printed in the United States of America.
ISBN-13: 978-1091763326
LCCN: 2019938176

Contents

Introduction

The Hamilton County Genealogical Society (HCGS) invites you to enjoy doing research in the superb Public Library of Cincinnati and Hamilton County and in other local genealogical repositories. We wish you much success in gathering information for your family history.

The latest edition of this guide features numerous updates, expanded information, reorganization by topic, cross-references to the HCGS website and how-to articles in the HCGS journal, and new information about Jewish records, census records, German records, naturalization records, orphan asylum records, tax lists and indexes, and online resources.

Many area residents and HCGS members are descendants of pioneers who came to the Northwest Territory. A group of 26 colonists from New Jersey and Pennsylvania led by Major Benjamin Stites landed 18 November 1788 at Columbia, a second group landed 28 December 1788 in what is now Cincinnati, and a third group of 14 colonists landed 2 February 1789 at North Bend, Ohio. John Cleves Symmes was prominent among New Jersey men who, as partners, purchased the original large tract of land on the north side of the Ohio River and between the Great Miami and Little Miami Rivers. Cincinnati soon became the capital of the Territory, and by 1794 (after the defeat of the Indian tribes further north in Ohio), this whole region was safe for settlement.

Hamilton County (originally encompassing a much larger area) was officially established in 1790 and named in honor of the Secretary of the U.S. Treasury, Alexander Hamilton. John Filson, a schoolmaster and surveyor from Kentucky, originally named the town in 1788. It was named Losantiville from the letter L for the Licking River, the Latin word *os* for mouth, the Greek word *anti* for across from, and the French word *ville* for city, or the city across from the mouth of the Licking River. The town was renamed Cincinnati in 1790 by Governor/General Arthur St. Clair after the Order of the Cincinnati organized in 1783 on the banks of the Hudson River in New York for officers in the Revolutionary War. The Society was named after a famous Roman soldier, Lucius Quintus Cincinnatus. Ohio became the seventeenth state of the United States in 1803.

The greatest numbers of early settlers in Hamilton County were from Pennsylvania, New Jersey, New York, Massachusetts, Maryland, Connecticut, and Virginia. Europeans came from England, Ireland, and the German states, but starting in the 1840s even greater numbers of German and Irish immigrants arrived. After 1880, numerous Italians came to Hamilton County as well as eastern Europeans, many of Jewish heritage. African American families lived in Cincinnati in its early years, and after World War I, many southern families came here to find work and better living conditions. For the same reasons, people from the Appalachian regions arrived here in the 1950s. Still later, many people of Asian backgrounds made Cincinnati their home. Thus, Cincinnati and its surrounding area is peopled by a rich diversity of heritages.

The Hamilton County Genealogical Society was chartered in 1973 with twelve members. In 2018, HCGS celebrated its 45th anniversary with 1,100 members. HCGS offers a variety of educational and interesting programs each year and participates in several projects and activities. HCGS sponsors an annual seminar and publishes books; a digital newsletter, *The Gazette*; and an award-winning quarterly periodical, *The Tracer*. HCGS sponsors special interest groups focusing on special research in German, Irish, and Jewish heritage as well as DNA and technology. In addition, HCGS honors members whose ancestors lived in Hamilton County before 31 December 1820 through its First Families of Hamilton County program, those whose ancestors were in Hamilton County between 1 January 1821 and 31 December 1860 through its Settlers and Builders program, and Century Families for those documenting ancestors in Hamilton County between 1 January 1861 and 100 years ago from today.

If you are interested in the Hamilton County Genealogical Society, write or phone for a membership brochure or visit the website. You may also write to the HCGS Research Committee, requesting information or a list of local professional researchers. We are happy to provide you with a complete array of genealogical services. Stay connected with us on Facebook, Twitter, and our blog.

Connie Stunkel Christman and Kenny R. Burck

Hamilton County Genealogical Society

Contributors

Adele Blanton	Pam Minning
Paul Cauthen	Sandra Morgan
Rick Cauthen	Eileen Muccino
Nancy Chouteau	Jean Nathan
Deb Cyprych	Bob Rau
Jim Dempsey	Kathy Reed
Bill Graver	Mary Remler
Jeff Herbert	Julie Ross
Carol Mahan	

Contact the Hamilton County Genealogical Society at (513) 956-7078; info@hcgsohio.org; or P. O. Box 15865, Cincinnati, OH 45215-0865. The website is https://hcgsohio.org.

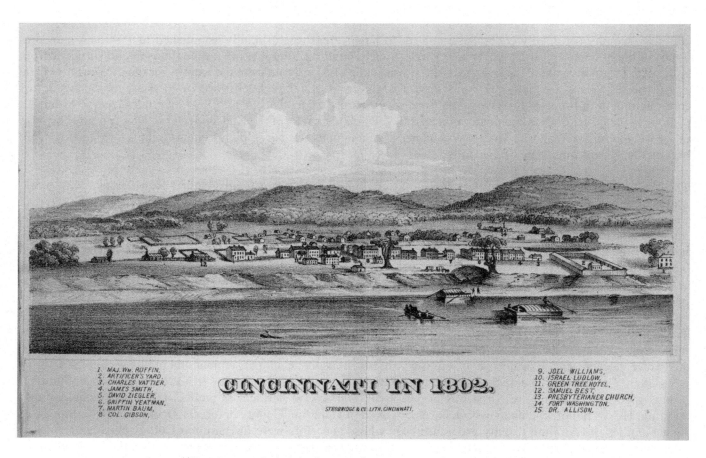

1. MAJ. Wm. RUFFIN,
2. ARTIFICER'S YARD,
3. CHARLES VATTIER,
4. JAMES SMITH,
5. DAVID ZIEGLER,
6. GRIFFIN YEATMAN,
7. MARTIN BAUM,
8. COL. GIBSON,

9. JOEL WILLIAMS,
10. ISRAEL LUDLOW,
11. GREEN TREE HOTEL,
12. SAMUEL BEST,
13. PRESBYTERIANER CHURCH,
14. FORT WASHINGTON,
15. DR. ALLISON.

CINCINNATI IN 1802.

STROBRIDGE & CO. LITH. CINCINNATI.

https://libraries.uc.edu/arb/collections/urban-studies/cincinnati-maps.html

Chapter 1: Repositories

Public Library of Cincinnati and Hamilton County

800 Vine Street (8th & Vine), Cincinnati, OH 45202-2071

(513) 369-6905 (Genealogy and Local History Dept.)

Hours: M-W 9-9, TH-F-SA 9-6, SU 1-5

www.cincinnatilibrary.org

The Public Library of Cincinnati and Hamilton County (PLCH) houses one of the largest genealogical collections in the United States, with many records for all states and strong resources for German, Irish, and African American research needs. The Library has more than 100,000 genealogy books, 1,500 genealogy periodicals, over 50,000 microfilms, more than 250,000 microfiches, and more than 12,000 family histories.

Ancestry Library Edition is available in all PLCH branch libraries. The Digital Library offers city directories, historical books, yearbooks, magazine and newspaper articles, and many other resources. The Research and Homework section of the PLCH website (Research Databases > Genealogy) includes African American Heritage, Fold3, HeritageQuest, and several newspapers (see page 60). Some resources require a PLCH library card.

COLLECTION	DESCRIPTION	DATES	FORMAT	PLACE
Census	All states available	1790-1940, all states (1890, very limited)	Microfilm	3rd Floor - Genealogy & Local History Dept.
Soundex/Miracode	All available states	1880-1920 (except 1890) & part of 1930	Microfilm	
Mortality Census	Ohio and others	Various	Book & Film	
Veterans Census	Ohio and others	1890	Book & Film	
Census Index	Hamilton County	1820-1880	Book	
Agricultural Census	Hamilton County	1850-1870	Microfilm	
Industry Census	Hamilton County	1850 & 1870-1880	Microfilm	
Defective Dependent Delinquent Schedules	Hamilton County	1880	Microfilm	
Passenger List Indexes	Baltimore	1820-1952	Microfilm	3rd Floor - Genealogy & Local History Dept.
	Baltimore (City)	1833-1866 (Supplemental)	"	
	Boston	1848-1891; 1902-1920	"	
*St. Albans District covers entire Canadian border crossings from Maine to the Great Lakes	Galveston	1896-1906	"	
	Gulfport, MS	1904-1954	"	
	New Bedford, MA	1902-1954	"	
	New York	1820-1846; 1897-1943	"	
	New Orleans	1853-1952	"	
	Other Atlantic & Gulf Ports	1820-1874 (Supplemental)	"	
	Pascagoula, MS	1903-1935	"	
	Philadelphia	1800-1926	"	
	St. Albans, VT*	1895-1924	"	
	San Francisco	1893-1934	"	
	Various	Ask Librarian	Book	

COLLECTION	DESCRIPTION	DATES	FORMAT	PLACE
Passenger Lists of Vessels (Actual Lists)	Baltimore Boston New Bedford, MA New Orleans New York Philadelphia	1820-1891 1820-1891 1902-1942 1820-1902 1820-1904 1800-1882	Microfilm " " " " "	3rd Floor - Genealogy & Local History Dept.
City Directories	Most Large Cities in U.S. (Cincinnati 1819 to present)	Various Years See additional information on pages 49-50	Cincinnati in book, film, & website. Other cities on film only	3rd Floor - Genealogy & Local History Dept.
City of Cincinnati Death Records		1865-1876 & 1878-1908 1865-1877 & 1878-1908	Microfilm Book	3rd Floor - Genealogy & Local History Dept.
Cincinnati Newspapers See list on pages 59-60	Enquirer Post Times-Star Post & Times-Star Commercial Gazette	1841-present 1882-1958 1840-1958 1958-present 1858-1899** 1827-1881**	Film & Website Film & Website " " " "	2nd Floor - South Building Magazines & Newspapers
Cincinnati Newspaper Index	Obituaries Death Notices News Articles	From 1940s From 1980s Starts in 1811 (incomplete)	Computer	Newsdex on PLCH website
Cincinnati German Newspapers See list on pages 59-60	Volksblatt Volksfreund Freie Presse Cincinnatier Zeitung	1846-1918** 1850-1908** 1874-1920** 1887-1901**	Microfilm " " "	2nd Floor - South Building Magazines & Newspapers
Ohio Death Records: Index Certificates Stillborn Certificates	All Counties in Ohio	 1908-1954 1908-1953 1918-1944 & 1947-1953	 Microfilm " "	3rd Floor - Genealogy & Local History Dept.
Church, Cemetery & Funeral Home Records See list on pages 23-26	Mostly Protestant Churches		Microfilm	3rd Floor - Genealogy & Local History Dept.
Local History & Surname Index	Index of various genealogy & local history books	Various Years	Card File	3rd Floor - Genealogy & Local History Dept.
Hamilton County Records Indexes	Cinti. Birth Records Protestant Baptisms Church Death Records Naturalization Records Wills	1874-1875 Early-1899 1811-1889 1837-1916 1791-1901	Book " " " "	3rd Floor - Genealogy & Local History Dept.
Hamilton County Indexes to Deeds & Mortgage Transfers	By Area	1789-1903	Microfilm	3rd Floor - Genealogy & Local History Dept.

** Published HCGS index of deaths and other notices.

COLLECTION	DESCRIPTION	DATES	FORMAT	PLACE
Hamilton County Property Owners Cadastral Maps	Ask librarian for assistance	1847, 1869, & 1884 1856	Book Microfiche	3rd Floor - Genealogy & Local History Dept.
Sanborn Fire Insurance Maps	All of Ohio and adjacent states (and other locations)	1887-1950	Microfilm & Website	3rd Floor - Genealogy & Local History Dept.
Maps	160,000+ Third largest library collection in U.S.			3rd Floor - Genealogy & Local History Dept.
U.S. Geological Survey Maps	All states available	1789-1903	Microfilm	3rd Floor - Genealogy & Local History Dept.
Hamilton County Probate Court Records	Applications for Administration	1884-1973	Microfilm	3rd Floor - Genealogy & Local History Dept.
"	Applications for Minor Guardianship	1884-1897	Microfilm	3rd Floor - Genealogy & Local History Dept.
"	Birth Records & Index	1863-1908	Microfilm	3rd Floor - Genealogy & Local History Dept.
"	Death Records	1882-1890; 1893-1908	Microfilm	3rd Floor - Genealogy & Local History Dept.
"	Guardianship Docket Records with Index	1852-1900	Microfilm	3rd Floor - Genealogy & Local History Dept.
"	Account & Inventory Records of Estates	1884-1917; Scattered years 1809-1882	Microfilm	3rd Floor - Genealogy & Local History Dept.
"	Marriage Banns	1883-1905, 1929, 1938	Microfilm	3rd Floor - Genealogy & Local History Dept.
"	Marriage Indexes (Arranged chronologically by Surname, First name)	1817-1962	Microfilm	3rd Floor - Genealogy & Local History Dept.
"	Probate Entries (Accounts & Petitions for sale of real estate)	1834-1837	Microfilm	3rd Floor - Genealogy & Local History Dept.
"	Will Indexes Wills	1791-1900 1860-1880, 1885	Microfilm	3rd Floor - Genealogy & Local History Dept.
Military Service of Ohioans	Civil War, Mexican War, Spanish-American War, WWI		Books	3rd Floor - Genealogy & Local History Dept.
General Index to Pension Records	Mostly Union Pension & Service Records for all Union States & Areas	1861-1934	Microfilm	3rd Floor - Genealogy & Local History Dept.

COLLECTION	DESCRIPTION	DATES	FORMAT	PLACE
Veteran Grave Registration Cards	Organized by Cemetery	America's Early Wars to Vietnam (incomplete)	Index Cards	3rd Floor - Genealogy & Local History Dept.
Draper Manuscript Collection	Various eastern states and the entire Ohio River valley	ca. 1755-1815	Microfilm	3rd Floor - Genealogy & Local History Dept.
Ohio WWI Draft Registration Cards	All counties in Ohio	1917-1918	Microfilm	3rd Floor - Genealogy & Local History Dept.

Surname File

The Public Library of Cincinnati and Hamilton County maintains a Surname File. Ask a librarian to retrieve the alphabetized file, which is arranged in several wooden file card drawers. Most cards contain information on Hamilton County families.

Local History Card File

This card file in the Genealogy and Local History Department indexes numerous histories. The card file has been completely digitized and posted in the PLCH Digital Library at http://goo.gl/J30Qwt.

Cincinnati Room

The Joseph S. Stern, Jr. Cincinnati Room, adjacent to the Genealogy and Local History Department, displays local history artifacts and provides a climate-controlled and secure environment for using the Library's rare and fragile materials. The collection of manuscripts and rare books is particularly strong in Cincinnati and Ohio River Valley history and culture. Unique materials include the Inland Rivers Library and a large postcard collection, among many other items in closed stacks. Hours: M-F 9-5 p.m., SA 9-6 p.m., SU 1-5 p.m.

Digital Library

PLCH offers a rapidly growing collection of online resources at no charge through its Digital Library, https://digital.cincinnatilibrary.org. Featured collections include Genealogy & Local History, City & County Directories, Yearbooks, Cincinnati Businesses, Maps & Atlases, and many more. For the full list and articles on using the Digital Library, see page 86.

Public Library of Cincinnati and Hamilton County Call Numbers

The Dewey Decimal System is used to catalog its books. Listed below are call numbers for historical and genealogical materials and related topics of interest to the Hamilton County researcher.

016.929105	PERSI (Periodical Source Index)
016.92934347	Emigration Lists
200s	Religion
282	Roman Catholic
283	Anglican
284	Lutheran, Calvinistic, Moravian, Huguenot, and Anabaptist
285	Presbyterian & Congregationalist
286	Baptist
287	Methodist
289	Church of Christ, Quaker, and Mormon
296	Judaism
305.8	African Americans
325	Some Passenger Lists
340	Laws and Court Cases
909.04	History of Ethnic Groups
911 & 912	Atlases
917	City of Cincinnati Books
929.1	Works about Genealogy (How-to Books)
929.2	Family Histories
929.3	Genealogy Sources, Census, &

	County Records, etc. (including other Hamilton County books)
929.308 & 309	Some Passenger Records
929.373 & 374	Some Passenger Records
929.37717	Hamilton County Genealogical Sources
929.37	Census Indexes
929.3771	Ohio Census Indexes
929.4	Names
929.5	Cemetery Records
929.502573	Cemeteries of the U.S.
929.509771	Hamilton County Cemetery Records
929.5097717	Hamilton County Cemetery Records
940	European History
940.9209 036	Roster of Ohio Soldiers WWI 1917-1918
970	General History of North America (various groups)
973	U.S. History
973.0042	Book of Emigrants
973.1	Pre-1607 Wars
973.2	Colonial Period 1607-1775
973.3	American Revolution 1775-1789 & Confederation Period
973.34	Abstracts of Revolutionary War Pension Files
973.4 to .6	Pre Civil War 1789-1861
973.52	Index to War of 1812 Pension Files
973.7	Civil War 1861-1865
973.742	Roster of Confederate Soldiers 1861-1865
973.7471	Roster of Ohio Soldiers 1861-1865
973.8	Reconstruction 1865-1901
973.9	After 1901 Wars
974.8	Pennsylvania
974.8P41	Pennsylvania Archives
974.9	New Jersey
975.2	Maryland
975.4	West Virginia
975.5	Virginia
975.6	North Carolina
975.8	Records of Ante-Bellum Plantations
976.8	Tennessee
976.9	Kentucky
977.1	Ohio
977.17	Cincinnati
977.2	Indiana

Hamilton County Courthouse, 1819-1849

Cincinnati History Library and Archives

Cincinnati Museum Center

1301 Western Avenue, Cincinnati, OH 45203

(513) 287-7030

Hours: M-F 12-5, SA 10-5

http://library.cincymuseum.org

The Cincinnati History Library and Archives (CHLA) was founded in 1831 as the library of the Historical and Philosophical Society of Ohio. It has been collecting and preserving materials relating to the greater Cincinnati area, the state of Ohio, and the history of the Northwest Territory ever since. The library is free and open to the public. CHLA's catalog has over 34,000 records, many of interest to genealogists.

Some materials are stored offsite. Request materials in advance of planned use so staff may have them ready upon arrival.

- Cincinnati and Hamilton County directories
- Marriage records, Methodist Episcopal Church (1861-1937)
- Index to annual reports of the Cincinnati Workhouse (1868-1890)
- Index to annual reports of the Old Men's Home of Cincinnati (1881-1930)
- Microfilm of indexes and documents of the Hamilton County Recorder's Office: deeds, mortgages, partnerships, powers of attorney, veteran discharges, deed indexes
- Microfilm copies of the federal population census of Ohio (1820-1840) and southwestern Ohio (1850-1930)
- Published family histories and state, county, and town histories of Ohio and other states
- Civil War regimental histories
- Over 11,000 manuscript collections, including the records of churches, businesses, family papers, tax records, cultural organizations, etc. See below for a list of manuscript collections of genealogical interest that have online indexes.
- 800,000 photographs of places and events of the Greater Cincinnati area including major events, transportation, buildings, parks, street scenes, businesses, people, etc., with some available online.
- 2,500 maps
- 140 newspaper titles, 300 periodical subscriptions
- The Digital Journals project is a searchable full-text database of seven journals (see list below) published by the Cincinnati Historical Society, the Cincinnati Museum Center, and the Cincinnati Museum of Natural History, with images of the original pages.
- At least 16 reference sources are currently indexed online, including *History of Hamilton County, Ohio; Christ Church;* and *Cincinnati's Colored Citizens*

Index of Local History Resources

The Index to Local History Resources is an index of names, places, and topics from Cincinnati reference books and other sources. The books and resources are available at the library. This database searches twenty-one sources by keyword or name.

Digital Journals

The following journals are available in a full-text database.

- *Quarterly Publication of the Historical and Philosophical Society of Ohio* (1906-1923)
- *Bulletin of the Historical and Philosophical Society of Ohio* (1943-1963)
- *Cincinnati Historical Society Bulletin* (1964-1982)
- *Queen City Heritage* (1983-1999)
- *Ohio Valley History* (2001-2006)*
- *Cincinnati Quarterly Journal of Science* (1874-1875)
- *Journal of the Society of Cincinnati Natural History* (1878-1945)

Back issues of most of the history journals are available for purchase from the Cincinnati History Library and Archives.

*Issues of the current journal (*Ohio Valley History*) from 2007 forward have not been digitized. Print copies are available for purchase.

Online indexes of genealogical manuscripts

Finding aids for manuscript collections vary in the details they contain. Some collections of genealogical interest have been updated to include individual names, thanks to the efforts of the staff and volunteers at the Cincinnati History Library and Archives. The following manuscripts contain name lists that are searchable online in Archives and Manuscripts on the website.

- American Red Cross, Cincinnati Chapter Records, 1905-2008, n.d. (not dated)
- Christ Church Records, 1821-1996
- Cincinnati Foundation for the Aged, 1888-1954, n.d.
- General (German) Protestant Orphan Home Records 1849-1973
- Hamilton County Genealogical Society Lineage Society Records
- Independent Order of Odd Fellows, Humboldt Lodge, No. 274 Records 1908-1922, n.d.
- Maple Knoll Hospital and Home Records (Home for the Friendless and Foundlings) 1854-1960
- New Orphan Asylum for Colored Children Records 1875-1967
- Ohio Court of Common Please Records, 1836-1858
- Price Hill United Church of Christ Records, 1885-2003
- St. Aloysius Orphanage Records 1837-2013
- Soldiers' Relief Commission of Hamilton County Burial Records, 1907-1958
- Woodward at War Scrapbooks

Tracer articles

- "Finding Aids: What They Are and How to Use Them," September 2017
- "Name Indexes in Online Manuscript Registers on Cincinnati History Library and Archives' Website," December 2018

Archives and Rare Books Library at the Carl Blegen Library, University of Cincinnati

8th floor, Blegen Library, 2602 McMicken Cir, Cincinnati, OH 45221

(513) 556-1959

Hours: M-F 8–5

www.libraries.uc.edu/libraries/arb

Inventory of Hamilton County Government Documents

The Archives and Rare Books Library is located on the eighth floor of the Blegen Library Building and can be reached from the fourth floor lobby via the elevator on the east side of the building. Below is a sample of records available. URLs and brief descriptions are given for digitized collections and online indexes.

OFFICE	COLLECTION	DATES
Court of Common Pleas	Record of Stray Animals	1825-1864
"	Civil Dockets 　Cincinnati Twp. 　Whitewater Twp.	 1846-1900 1860-1876
"	Criminal Dockets 　Cincinnati Twp. 　Delhi Twp. 　Millcreek Twp. 　Whitewater Twp.	 1860-1913 1853-1905 1853-1863 & 1881-1890 1860-1931
"	Apprenticeship Book 　Cincinnati Twp.	 1862-1898
Correctional Institute	Workhouse Records	1877-1915
Probate Court	Adoption Records (Restored)	ca. 1850-1884
"	Assignment Docket	1857-1877
"	Assignment Record	ca. 1884-1895
"	Journal Entry Books	1858-1904
"	Index to Marriages	1871-1873
"	Marriage Banns	1883-1889 & 1928-1931
"	Record of Births	1881-1908
"	Cinti. Birth Records*	1874-1908 w/card file index
"	Cinti. Death Records*	1865-1908 w/card file index
"	Citation Docket	1859-1892
"	Index to Admin. Dockets	1852-1884
"	Estate Records	ca. 1850-1900
"	Marriage Records (Restored)	1839-1902
"	Naturalization Records* (Declarations of Intent)	ca. 1837-1915
"	Naturalization Records* (Complete Record)	ca. 1865-1906

"	Wills (originals)*	1791-1901
"	Ministers' Licenses	ca. 1850-1900
"	Estate Packets	1906-1972 must have case # from probate court
County Coroner	Morgue Records	1887-1930
County Sheriff	Jail Registers	1834-1943
House of Refuge	Record of Commitments	1869-1882 & 1891-1902

*Partial published Hamilton County record indexes are available at the Archives and Rare Books Library and the Public Library of Cincinnati and Hamilton County.

Archives and Rare Books Library databases

Cincinnati Birth and Death Records, 1865-1912
http://digital.libraries.uc.edu/collections/birthdeath
Searchable images of 528,000 index cards created by the Cincinnati Health Department several decades ago and considered the official and legal records of births and deaths for this time period.

Civil War Exemptions
http://digital.libraries.uc.edu/collections/civilwar
Searchable images of military service exemptions granted by the Provost Marshal General's Bureau upon posting of a monetary bond.

Hamilton County, Ohio Citizenship Records
http://libraries.uc.edu/arb/collections/local-government/naturalization.html
Index to some of the original and restored declarations of intention to naturalize (ca. 1837-1915) and naturalization papers (ca. 1865-1906) filed in Hamilton County. See pages 53-58 for more information about locating naturalization records.

Hamilton County, Ohio Wills, 1791-1901
http://libraries.uc.edu/arb/collections/local-government/will-index.html
Index to the original wills of Hamilton County, containing testator's given name and surname, testator's place of residence, date filed in probate court, executors, beneficiaries, case number, box number.

Hamilton County Morgue Records, 1887-1930
http://digital.libraries.uc.edu/collections/morgue
Searchable images of morgue records. Details in the morgue records include the date, time, and location where the body was found; personal information on the deceased; probable cause of death; removal of the body; and sometimes effects found on the body. Data also transcribed into searchable spreadsheets.

House of Refuge Records
http://digital.libraries.uc.edu/collections/refuge
Searchable images of five volumes. Includes an index, financial records, and payroll records. The Record of Commitments (1869-1882, 1891-1902) includes the names of individuals committed, their nationality, a description of their offenses or the reason for admittance, information on their parents, and their age.

Chapter 2: Genealogical and Historical Books and Articles

City of Cincinnati and Hamilton County Histories
in chronological order of publication

Sources: B=PLCH book, BC=PLCH book that can be checked out, DL= PLCH digital library, G=Google Books, H=HathiTrust, IA=Internet Archive, M=PLCH microfilm, OL=openlibrary.org

Natural and Statistical View, or, Picture of Cincinnati and the Miami Country: Illustrated by Maps with an Appendix Containing Observations on the Late Earthquakes, the Aurora Borealis, and South-West Wind by Daniel Drake (1815, 1955 reprint) [B, M, DL, G]

Cincinnati in 1826 by Benjamin Drake and E. D. Mansfield (1827) [B, M, DL, G]

Cincinnati in 1841: Its Early Annals and Future Prospects by Charles Cist (1841) [M, DL]

Cincinnati Miscellany, or, Antiquities of the West, and Pioneer History and General and Local Statistics... by Charles Cist (1845-1846) [B, DL]

Sketches and Statistics of Cincinnati in 1851 by Charles Cist (1851) [B, M, DL, G, H, IA]

Sketches and Statistics of Cincinnati in 1859 by Charles Cist (1859), indexed by HCGS in 2001, at Cincinnati History Library & Archives [B, M, DL, G, IA]

Memoirs of the Life and Services of Daniel Drake, M.D., Physician, Professor, and Author; with Notices of the Early Settlement of Cincinnati and Some of its Pioneer Citizens by Edward D. Mansfield, LL.D. (1860) [B, M, DL, G]

The City of Cincinnati: A Summary of its Attractions, Advantages, Institutions and Internal Improvements by George E. Stevens (1869) [B, M, DL, G, H]

The Suburbs of Cincinnati: Sketches, Historical and Descriptive by Sidney Denise Maxwell (1870, 1974 reprint) [BC, DL, G, IA]

Pioneer Life in Kentucky, a Series of Reminiscential Letters from Daniel Drake, M.D., of Cincinnati, to His Children by Charles D. Drake (1870) [B, M, DL, G, IA]

Illustrated Cincinnati: A Pictorial Hand-book of the Queen City: Comprising its Architecture, Manufacture, Trade, its Social, Literary, Scientific and Charitable Institutions, its Churches, Schools, and Colleges, and All Other Principal Points of Interest to the Visitor and Resident, Together with an Account of the Most Attractive Suburbs by Daniel J. Kenny (1875, 1986 reprint) [BC, M, DL, IA]

Personal Memories, Social, Political, and Literary: with Sketches of Many Noted People, 1803-1843 by E.D. Mansfield (1879) [B, M, DL, G, H, IA, OL]

Reminiscences and Anecdotes of the Courts and Bar of Cincinnati by Judge Carter (1880) [B]

History of Hamilton County by Henry A. & Kate B. Ford (1881, 1974 and 1993 reprints), indexed by HCGS in 2002 [BC, G, IA, OL]

Picturesque Cincinnati by James W. Dawson (1883) [B, DL, H, IA]

Cincinnati Illustrated Business Directory by Spencer & Craig Printing Works (1882,1883,1885,1886, 1887,1888,1889,1890,1891,1892,1892,1893,1894,1895,1896,1897,1898,1899,1900,1902, 2017 Arcadia reprint) [BC, DL]

A Guide to Picturesque Cincinnati by W. W. Spooner, ed. (1883) [B]

Leading Manufacturers and Merchants of Cincinnati and Environs: The Great Railroad Centre of the South and Southwest: An Epitome of the City's History and Descriptive Review of the Industrial Enterprises (1886) [B, DL, H]

Thirty-five Years Among the Poor, and the Public Institutions of Cincinnati by Joseph Emery (1887) [B, DL]

Extracts from the History of Cincinnati and the Territory of Ohio: Showing the Trials and Hardships of the Pioneers in the Early Settlement of Cincinnati and the West by Adophus E. Jones (1888) [B, DL, H]

The Centennial Review of Cincinnati: Progress in Commerce, Manufactures, the Professions and in Social and Municipal Life by John Leonard (1888) [BC, DL]

History of Cincinnati & Hamilton County, Ohio... Includes Biographies and Portraits of Pioneer ... by S. B. Nelson (1894, 1993 reprint) [B, DL, H]

Cincinnati: The Queen City of the West: Her Principal Men and Institutions... by George M. Roe (1895) [BC, DL]

Hamilton County, Ohio: as Extracted from Henry Howe's Historical Collections of Ohio (1896), edited with new preface and introduction by Barbara Keyser Gargiulo (2005) [B]

Picturesque Cincinnati by Albert O. Kraemer (1898, 1903, 1985 reprint) [BC, DL]

Picturesque Cincinnati by Weisbrodt & Co. (1890, 1905) [B, DL]

Cincinnati, the Queen City by George Washington Engelhardt (1901, 1982 reprint) [BC, DL]

Centennial History of Cincinnati by Charles T. Greve (1904) - 2 Vol. [B, M, DL, IA, H], *Index to Greve's History of Cincinnati* by PLCH (1915) [B]

Cincinnati, The Queen City by Rev. Charles F. Goss (1912) - 4 Vol. [B, DL, IA, H]

Cincinnati, "the Queen City": newspaper reference book by Cuvier Press Club (1914) [B, DL]

The Bench and Bar of Cincinnati, Commemorating the Building of the New Court House. by Wm. W. Morris (1921) [B, DL, H]

Pioneers of Night Life on Vine Street: Vol. 1 Dedicated to the Old-timers of Cincinnati by Frank Y. Grayson (1924) [B]

Cincinnati's Colored Citizens: Historical, Sociological, and Biographical by Wendell P. Dabney (1926, 1970 and 1988 reprints) [BC]

Greater Cincinnati & Its People: A History by Lewis A. Leonard (1927) - 4 Vol. [B, H]

They Built a City: 150 Years of Industrial Cincinnati compiled and written by the Cincinnati Federal Writers' Project of the Work Progress Administration in Ohio (1938) [BC]

Cincinnati: Story of the Queen City by Clara Longworth De Chambrun (1939) [BC]

The WPA Guide to Cincinnati by Works Projects Administration and the City of Cincinnati, Ohio (1943). Also published as *Cincinnati: A Guide to the Queen City and its Neighbors* by The Cincinnati Historical Society (1987) [BC]

Cincinnati Then and Now by Iola Silberstein (1949, 1956, 1966, 1982) [BC]

The Serene Cincinnatians by Alvin Fay Harlow (1950) [BC]

Cincinnati in 1840: A Community Profile by Walter Stix Glazer (1968) [B]

Boss Cox's Cincinnati: Urban Politics in the Progressive Era by Zane L. Miller (1968, 1970, 1980, 1981, 2000) [BC]

Who Governed Cincinnati? A Comparative Analysis of Government and Social Structure in a Nineteenth Century River City: 1819-1860 by Irwin Flack (1981) [BC]

Workers on the Edge: Work, Leisure, and Politics in Industrializing Cincinnati, 1788-1890 by Steven J. Ross (1985) [BC]

The Bicentennial Guide to Greater Cincinnati: A Portrait of Two Hundred Years by Geoffrey J. Giglierano and Deborah A. Overmyer with Fred. L. Propas (1988) [BC]

Cincinnati: An Urban History Sourcebook by Cincinnati Historical Society (1988) - 2 Vol. [BC]

Plague of Strangers: Social Groups and the Origins of City Services in Cincinnati by Alan I. Marcus (1991) [BC]

Cincinnati: Queen City of the West 1819-1838 by Daniel Aaron (1992) [BC]

Cincinnati in 1840: The Social and Functional Organization of an Urban Community during the Pre-Civil War Period by Walter Stix Glazer (1999) [BC]

Frontiers of Freedom: Cincinnati's Black Community, 1802-1868 by Nikki M. Taylor (2005) [BC]

Cincinnati, The Queen City, 225th Anniversary Edition original text by Daniel Hurley, updated content by Paul A. Tenkotte (2014) [B]

Local Histories: Neighborhoods and Townships

Addyson – *Diary of an Historic Village, Addyston, OH 1891-1991* (1991) R977.177 qS623
Amberley Village – *Amberley Village, Its History and Its People* (1990) R977.177 A491
Anderson Township – *Township Tales: Some Peeks into the Past of People and Places in Anderson Township, Hamilton County, Ohio* (1988) R977.177 L917
Anderson Township – *Anderson Township Historical Society, Hamilton County, Ohio: The First 25 Years* (1992) R977.177 A552ZL
Anderson Township – *Historic Homes, Anderson Township, Hamilton County, Ohio* R977.177 qS635h v. 01
Anderson Township – *Now and Then in Anderson Township* (1987) R977.177 qS635N 1987
Blue Ash – *Celebrating Blue Ash in 2005: A Supplement to the History of Blue Ash, Ohio, 1793-1991* (2005) R977.177 qR797 1991 Suppl
Blue Ash – *Blue Ash History and Directory, 1793-1968* (1968) R977.177 K62
Blue Ash – *History of Blue Ash, Ohio, 1791-1991* (1991) R977.177 qR797 1991
Brighton – *Historic Brighton: Its Origin, Growth and Development* (1902) R977.178 M912 1902 (also Digital Library)
Camp Dennison – *The History of Camp Dennison, OH 1796-1956* (2003) R977.177 S634 1987
Clifton – *Clifton: Neighborhood and Community in an Urban Setting: A Brief History* (2014) R977.178 S529
Clifton – *Sights and Scenes of Clifton; An Historical Tour* (1965) 917.7199 S755
Colerain Township – *Our Heritage: Colerain Township* (1976) R977.178 092
Colerain Township – *Colerain Township "Revisited": 1794-1994 Bicentennial Year* (1994) R977.178 qW455 1994
Colerain Township – *A History of Colerain Township from Frontier Wilderness to Suburban Sprawl* (2018) R977.177 F447c
College Hill – *College Hill Centennial, 1866-1966...* (1966) R977.178 qC697
College Hill – *Old College Hill* (1982/1988) R977.178 O42
College Hill – *A Little Piece of Paradise, College Hill, Ohio* (1999) R977.178 qL778 1999
College Hill – *History of College Hill and Vicinity: With a Sketch of Pioneer Life in This Part of Ohio* (1886) R977.199 C33 (also Digital Library)
Columbia Township – *Glimpses into the Past; Tales of People, Settlements and Events Within Columbia, Symmes & Sycamore Townships, Hamilton County, Ohio* (1940) 977.199 K13g
Columbia Township – *Columbia Township, Hamilton County, Ohio Record Book: Selected Pages* (1934) 977.199 qC722 (also Digital Library)

Columbia Tusculum – *Columbia Tusculum 1788-1988* (1988) R977.178 C726 1988
Crosby Township – *The History of Crosby Township, Hamilton County, OH* (1990) R977.177 qM128
Crosby Township – *A Crosby Township History* (2003) R977.177 qC949
Crosby Township – *The Shakers of White Water, Ohio, 1823-1916* (2014) 289.809771 qS527 2014
Crosby Township – *Whitewater, Ohio, Village of Shakers, 1824-1916: Its History and its People* (1979) 977.177 qW594
Cumminsville – *A History of Cumminsville, 1792-1914* (1988) R977.178 qH673 1988
Deer Park – *The History of Deer Park, Ohio* (1976) R977.177 N713
Deer Park – *Deer Park, Ohio, Past to Present* (1987) R977.177 D312
Delhi Township – *The New Pioneers: The People of Delhi, 1830-1900* (1989) R977.177 qA467
Delhi Township – *The History of Delhi Township* (1976/1994) R977.177 qD813
Elmwood Place – *Elm Tree Days* (1946) R977.199 S39e
Evendale – *Village of Evendale: 1951-2001* (2001) R977.177 qM243
Glendale – *Glendale, Ohio, 1855-1955* (1955) R977.177 qF219
Glendale – *Glendale's Heritage, Glendale, Ohio* (1976) R977.177 qG558
Green Township – *Historical Sketch of Greene Township, Hamilton County, Ohio* (1882) R977.199 R32
Green Township – *A Bicentennial History of Green Township: Uncovering a Jewel in the Crown of the Queen City 1809-2009* (2011) R977.177 F447
Green Township – *Kuliga, the Pretty Land: The Colorful Story of Green Township, Hamilton County, Ohio* (1949) 977.199 qG798h
Greenhills – *Act of Congress, Greenhills, Ohio 1938-1976* R977.177 qL766
Greenhills – *Greenhills, Ohio: The Evolution of an American New Town* (1978) R307.76 L434
Harrison – *Harrison, Ohio; Century and Silver Celebration* (1975) R977.177 qH323
Harrison – *Harrison, Ohio 1850-2000* (2000) R977.177 qH323ha
Hyde Park – *Hyde Park in Its Glory, An Historical Sketch* (1998) R977.178 qH995 1998
Hyde Park – *Cincinnati's Hyde Park: A Queen City Gem* (2010) R977.178 R726
Indian Hill – *Hither and Yon on Indian Hill* (1962) R977.177 qW588f 2001
Indian Hill – *Treasured Landmarks of Indian Hill* (1993) R977.177 qW588 1993
Indian Hill – *From Camargo to Indian Hill* (1983) (2001) R977.199 qI39W
Loveland – *Loveland: Passages Through Time* (1992) R977.177 qB442
Loveland – *Loveland, Ohio: The Story of a Town from its Beginning* (1976) R977.1794 qR475
Loveland – *The Loveland Story* (1963) R977.195 L898
Mariemont – *John Nolen and Mariemont: Building a New Town in Ohio* (2001) 711.409771 N791Zr
Mariemont – *The Mariemont Story: A National Exemplar in Town Planning* (1967) R977.177 P252
Mariemont – *A Dream Come True: A Brief History of Mariemont, "A National Exemplar"* (2000) R977.177 H646 2000
Miami Township – *Miami Township, Hamilton County, Ohio: Oyo and la Roche Rivers Historic Area* (2000) R977.177 qD778m 2000
Miami Township – *It Happened 'Round North Bend: A History of Miami Township and Its Borders* (1970) R977.177 qB969
Miami Township – *Miami Township, 1791-1991: A Taste of History* (1991) R977.177 B969m
Miami Township – *Dates of Interest to Miami Township: A Chronological History of the Community* (1987) 977.177 B969d
Mill Creek Valley – *The Past & Present of Mill Creek Valley: Being a Collection of Historical and Descriptive Sketches...* (1882/1993) R977.177 T258 1993 (also Digital Library)
Monfort Heights – *Remember When: Monfort Heights* (1977) R977.178 qR386 1977
Montgomery – *Ole' Montgomery, 1967: History and Directory, 1795-1967* (1967) R977.177 M788
Montgomery – *History of Montgomery, Ohio, 1795-1995* (1995) R977.177 qR7972c
Montgomery – *Ole' Montgomery: The Village of Lovely Homes and Friendly People...* (1960) 977.199 M788
Mount Airy – *Remembering Mount Airy: A Turn-of-the-Century Portrait* (1980) R977.178 M958
Mount Healthy – *Once Upon a Hilltop: June 7, 8, 9, 10, 11; Mount Healthy Area Sesqui-centennial, 1817-1967* (1967) R977.177 qO58
Mount Healthy – *One Square Mile: 1817-1992* (1992) R977.177 qO58s

Mount Lookout – *Mt. Lookout Centennial, 1870-1970* (1970) R917.7178 qM928

Mount Lookout – *Mt. Lookout 1870-1995: Celebrating 125 Years* (1995) R917.7178 qM928L 1995

Mount Washington – *A History of Mt. Washington: A Suburb of Cincinnati, Ohio* (1971) R977.178 qS635 1971

Mount Washington – *A Village is Born: Mt. Washington* (1968) R977.178 S365v

Newtown - *Newtown, Ohio, 200th Anniversary: Bicentennial Edition, 1792-1992* (1992) R977.177 qN567 1992

North Bend – (See Miami Township)

Northside – *Northside: A Walk through Neighborhood History* (1990) 917.717804 N877

Norwood – *Norwood, Her Homes and Her People: Pleasant Places...* (1988) R977.177 qM955 1988

Norwood – *The City of Norwood, Ohio, 1809-1957* (1957) 977.199 qN89

Norwood – *Norwood, Ohio: A Bicentennial Remembrance* (1976) R977.177 N895

Norwood – *Norwood, Ohio, 1787-1915* (1970) R977.177 qC536

Norwood – *A History of Norwood, Ohio* (1940) 977.177 qH6734

Over-The-Rhine – *Cincinnati, Over-The-Rhine: A Historical Guide to 19th Century Buildings and Their Residents* (1987) R977.178 qW757

Over-The-Rhine – *Over-The-Rhine, A Description and History...* (1995) R977.178 qY69 1995

Price Hill – *Price Hill: Preserving Yesterday, Today, for Tomorrow* (1990) R977.178 qP946

Price Hill – *Price Hill, Its Beauties & Advantages as a Place of Residence, 1894* (1998) R977.178 qP9461 1998

Price Hill – *Anthology of Price Hill History: A Gift...* (199-) R977.178 qA628

Pleasant Ridge – *A Bicentennial History of Pleasant Ridge, 1795-1995...* (1995) r977.178 Qd877 1995

Reading – *The History of Reading, Ohio: An American History* (1992) R977.177 qR162

Reading – *Reading, Ohio Sesquicentennial: 1851-2001* (2001) R977.177 qR287 2001

Rossmoyne – *Rossmoyne from Yesterday to ...1971* (1973) R977.178 qS779

St. Bernard – *Fifty Years of Progress, 1878, St. Bernard, Ohio, 1928* (1928) R977.199 S13

St. Bernard – *St. Bernard, Ohio, 1878-1978* (1978) R977.177 qN676

Sayler Park – *Pictures That Must be Seen—Life in Sayler Park: and More Saylor Park Stories* (2014) 977.1780922 qS884p

Sharonville – *Sharonville Then and Now* (1988) R977.177 qS531

Sharonville – *Sharonville Then & Now* (1991) R977.177 qS531 Every Name Index

Sycamore Township, Symmes Township – (See Columbia Township)

Terrace Park – *A Place Called Terrace Park* (1992) R977.177 R261

Terrace Park – *Terrace Park: From Unsettled Lands to Incorporation, 1789-1893* (2007) R977.177 qC689

Walnut Hills – *Walnut Hills, City Neighborhood* (1983) R977.178 W217

Westwood – *Westwood in Ohio: Community, Continuity, and Change* (1981) R977.178 K77 1981

White Oak – *Welcome to White Oak* (1988) R977.177 qN974

Winton Place – *Winton Place Historic Sites, 1989-1990* (1990) R977.178 W226 1990

Winton Place – *Memories of Winton Place: A History* (2011) R977.178 qM533

Wyoming – *Wyoming Centennial* (1974) R977.177 qW992

Wyoming – *Wyoming: A Retrospective* (2002) R977.177 qG921

The following books from the Arcadia Publishing series contain mainly illustrations:

Anderson Township - *Anderson Township, Anderson Township Historical Society* (2018) 977.177 A552

Colerain Township - *Colerain Township* (2010) R977.177 S368

College Hill - *College Hill* (2004) R977.178 F499

Green Township - *Hamilton County's Green Township* (2006) R977.177 L948

Greenhills - *Greenhills* (2013) R977.177 M657

Miami Township - *Miami Township* (2004) R977.172 M618

Mount Healthy - *Mt. Healthy* (2008) R977.177 W753

Northside - *Cincinnati's Northside Neighborhood* (2009) R977.178 W842

Over-The-Rhine - *Cincinnati's Over-the-Rhine* (2003) 977.17800222 G729c

Price Hill - *Price Hill* (2008) R977.178 S356

St. Bernard - *St. Bernard* (2011) R977.177 N676s

Sharonville - *Sharonville and its People* (2002) R977.177 E19

Wyoming - *Wyoming* (2005) R977.177 J68

The Hamilton County Genealogical Society's Publications

Baptism records

Hamilton County, Ohio Roman Catholic Baptism Records, Early-1849 by Jeffrey G. Herbert (2018)
Hamilton County, Ohio Roman Catholic Baptism Records, 1850-1859 Part 1: A-L, Part 2: M-Z by Jeffrey G. Herbert and Julie M. Ross (2018)
Hamilton County, Ohio Roman Catholic Baptism Records - Early – 1859 Excluding Hamilton County by Jeffrey G. Herbert and Julie M. Ross (2019)
Selected Hamilton County, Ohio Church Baptism Records (Protestant) by Jeffrey G. Herbert
- *Early to 1859* (2003)
- *1860-1869* (2004)
- *1870-1879* (2005)
- *1880-1889* (2007)
- *1890-1899* (2007)

Burial records

Hamilton County, Ohio Burial Records, edited by Mary H. Remler (except as noted)
- Vol. 1 – *Wesleyan Cemetery, 1842-1971 (Methodist Episcopal)* (1984)
- Vol. 2 – *Anderson Township Cemeteries, 1800-1989* (1990)
- Vol. 3 – *Vine Street Hill Cemetery, 1852-1977 (German Protestant)* (1991)
- Vol. 4 – *Miami Township Cemeteries* (1993)
- Vol. 5 – *Crosby & Whitewater Township Cemeteries* (1993)
- Vol. 6 – *Colerain Township Cemeteries* (1994)
- Vol. 7 – *Springfield Township Cemeteries* (1994)
- Vol. 8 – *Sycamore Township Cemeteries* (1994)
- Vol. 9 – *Union Baptist African American Cemetery*, 2 Vol. by Eleanor Dooks Bardes and Mary H. Remler (1997)
- Vol. 10 – *Green Township Cemeteries* (1998)
- Vol. 11 – *Columbia Township Cemeteries* (1998)
- Vol. 12 – *Calvary Cemetery* (1999)
- Vol. 13 – *First German Protestant Cemetery of Avondale & Martini United Church of Christ Records* by Jeffrey G. Herbert (2000)
- Vol. 14 – *Harrison Township* by Hazel L. Berry and Mary H. Remler (2000)
- Vol. 15 – *Walnut Hills United Jewish Cemetery, 1850-2002* by Anita Marks and Mary H. Remler (2003)
- Vol. 16 – *Walnut Hills (Originally German Protestant Cemetery), 1843-1993* by Jeffrey G. Herbert (2005)
- Vol. 17 – *Delhi Township Cemeteries, 1800's-2004* (2005)
- Vol. 18 – *New St. Joseph Irish Cemetery, 1850-1894* by Jeffrey G. Herbert (2008)
- Vol. 19 – *Old St. Joseph German Cemetery, 1845-1879* by Jeffrey G. Herbert (2009)
- Vol. 20 – *St. John German Cemetery, 1849-1879* by Jeffrey G. Herbert (2010)
- Vol. 21 – *Symmes Township Cemetery Index, 1800s-2012* by Mary H. Remler and Carol A. Sims (2013)
- Vol. 22 – *Baltimore Pike Cemetery, 1853-2010 (German Protestant)* by James G. Dempsey (2014)
- CD: Vol. 1 - 9, *Hamilton County Cemeteries* (1998)
- CD: Vol. 3 Vine Street Hill Cemetery and Vol. 16 Walnut Hills Cemetery

Church burial records

Hamilton County, Ohio Church Death Records 1811-1849 by Jeffrey G. Herbert (2000)
Hamilton County, Ohio, Church Burial Records by Jeffrey G. Herbert
- *1850-1859* (2000)
- *1860-1869* (2000)
- *1870-1879* (2001)
- *1880-1889* (2006)
- *1890-1899* (2016)

Court records

Abstract of Book 1 and Book A, Probate Record, 1791-1826 (1977)
Abstract of Book 3, Probate Record, 1829-1834, Hamilton County, Ohio (1981)
Abstract of Book 4, Probate Record, 1834-1837, Hamilton County, Ohio (1985)
Will Index of Hamilton County, Ohio, 1792-1850 (1975)
Wills Filed, Probate Court. Hamilton County, Ohio 1791 thru 1852 (1988)
Wills Filed, Probate Court. Hamilton County, Ohio Book 2 1853 thru1866 (1989)
CD: Abstract of Book 1, 3, and 4 Probate Records 1791-1837

Death records

Hamilton County, Ohio and Cincinnati, Ohio Morgue Records: June 1887-1992 by Margie and Michael Mohr (2004)
Index to Cincinnati, Ohio Death Records by Kenny R. Burck, Jean Overmeier Nathan, and Doris Thomson (except as noted)
- *1878-1881* (2010)
- *1882-1884* (2007)
- *1885-1887* (2006)
- *1888-1890* (2005)
- *1891-1893* (2004)
- *1894-1896* (2003)
- *1900-1902* (2006)
- *1903-1905* by Kenny R. Burck, Doris Thomson, and Marilyn Wood Armstrong (2003)
- *1906-1908* by Kenny R. Burck and Doris Thomson (2003)
- Volume of 1897-1899 death records was not published but is available at PLCH (Main) Library and Family History Center (Norwood) Library

Funeral home records

Barrere Funeral Home Records, 1927-1953 by Margie S. Thomas (1994)

Marriage records

Restored Hamilton County, Ohio Marriages by Jeffrey G. Herbert
- *1808-1849* (1998)
- *1850-1859* (1998)
- *1860-1869* (1997)
- *1870-1884* (1994)
- *1850-1884 Supplement* (2002)

Newspaper indexes

These indexes were compiled by Jeffrey G. Herbert.

Index of Death and Marriage Notices Appearing in the Cincinnati Enquirer *1818-1869* (2013)
Index of Death and Other Notices Appearing in the Cincinnati Freie Presse *1874-1920* (1993)
Index of Death Lists Appearing in the Cincinnatier Zeitung *1887-1901* (1999)
Index of Death, Marriage and Miscellaneous Notices Appearing in the Liberty Hall and Cincinnati Gazette *1804-1857* (2014)
Index of Death Notices Appearing in the Cincinnati Commercial *1858-1899* (1996)
Index of Death Notices Appearing in the Cincinnati Daily Times *1840-1879* (1994)
Index of Death Notices Appearing in Der Christliche Apologete, *1839-1899* (2016)
Index of Death Notices and Marriage Notices Appearing in the Cincinnati Daily Gazette *1827-1881* (1993)
Index of Death Notices and Marriage Notices Appearing in the Cincinnati Volksblatt *1846-1918* (1997)
Index of Death Notices and Marriage Notices Appearing in the Cincinnati Volksfreund *1850-1908* (1991)
Index of Hamilton County, Ohio Reported Court Records [Cincinnati Enquirer]
- *1841-1869* (2017)
- *1870-1879* (2018)
- *1880-1884* (2019)

Index of Notices Appearing in 23 Early Cincinnati Newspapers 1793-1853 (2015)

Other publications

First Families of Hamilton County, Ohio: Official Roster Vol. I 1988-1992, Vol. II 1993-1997
Index of Lesser Known German Resources by Marilyn Armstrong, Beverly Breitenstein, and Jeffrey G. Herbert (2013)
Index to Hamilton County, Ohio, Special Census: 1890 Union Veterans & Widows of the Civil War by Kenny R. Burck and Kay M. Ryan (2006)
CD or DVD: 30 Years of *The Tracer* and *The Gazette* 1979-2008

HCGS publications are available at the Public Library of Cincinnati & Hamilton County (Main Library) and at several branch libraries, including Anderson Township, Green Township, Madeira, and North Central.

See the websites of the Hamilton County Genealogical Society (https://hcgsohio.org/forsale.php), Heritage Books, Inc. (www.heritagebooks.com), or Little Miami Publishing Co. (www.littlemiamibooks.com) for information about the purchase of many Hamilton County books.

Other Hamilton County Genealogical Books

Available at the Public Library of Cincinnati and Hamilton County
or the Cincinnati History Library and Archives (noted as CHLA)

Birth, marriage, and death records

A Collection of Pioneer Marriage Records, Hamilton County, Ohio 1789-1817 by Marjorie Byrnside Burress (n.d.)

Deaths in the Annual Reports of the City Infirmary...July 1852-December 1891 (excluding 1882) by Chris Bell-Puckett (2001) CHLA

Deaths in the Annual Reports of the Cincinnati Hospital, 1868-1883 by Chris Bell-Puckett (2006) CHLA

Hamilton County Death Records by Lois E. Hughes (1992)
- Vol. 1 1865-1869
- Vol. 2 1870-1873
- Vol. 3 1874-1877

Hamilton County, Ohio Birth Records (1874-1875) by Lois E. Hughes (1993)

Hamilton County, Ohio Marriage Index (1817-1845) by Lois E. Hughes (1994)

Hamilton County, Ohio Records: Pioneers, Marriages, Deaths by Robert D. Craig (1964)

Marriages Recorded in Hamilton County, Ohio by Kenny R. Burck
- *1870-1884* (2006)
- *1885-1889* (2005)
- *1890-1894* (2006)
- *1895-1899* (2009)

Census records

1870 Census Index: to Hamilton County, Ohio Including Cincinnati by Pamela Miller and Richard Rees (1988)

Census for Cincinnati, Ohio, 1817: and Hamilton County, Ohio, Voters' Lists 1798-1799 by Marie Dickoré (1960)

First Census of the United States, 1790: Ohio North West Territorial Census Index by Ronald Vern Jackson (1984)

Ohio 1800 Census Index, 2 Vol. by Ronald Vern Jackson (1986)

Ohio 1830 Census Index by Ronald Vern Jackson (1976)

Ohio 1840 Federal Census Index by Ronald Vern Jackson (1981)

Ohio 1850 Census Index, 2 Vol. by Ronald Vern Jackson (1978)

Ohio 1850 Mortality Census Index by Ronald Vern Jackson (1979)

Ohio-South West 1860 Federal Census Index by Ronald Vern Jackson (1988)

The Black and Mulatto Population of Hamilton County, Ohio and the Cincinnati Additions but Excluding the City of Cincinnati as Taken from the Censuses of 1870 and 1860 Respectively by Audrey C. Werle (1980)

Church and funeral home records

Argo Records, Cleves, Ohio (Argo-Bolton & Lunsford Funeral Home Records) by George C. Dreyer (1992)
- Vol. 1 1845-1944
- Vol. 2 1944-1972

Funerals, 1854-1936, Conducted from Martini United Church of Christ... by Robert C. Rau (1981)

List of Names of Members of the Old Columbia Church (Baptist, 1790-1911) by Alfred R. Marsh (1941)

Minutes 1790-1825; List of Members 1808; June 20, 1890, Confession of Faith by Columbia Baptist Church (n.d. handwritten, no index)

T.P. White & Sons Funeral Home Index, Cincinnati, Ohio, 1935-1976 by Kenny R. Burck (2006)

Newspaper extracts

Catalog of 1,200+ Births, Marriages, Deaths, Burials & Biographical Sketches in the Weekly Issues of the Harrison News, Harrison, Ohio: December 23, 1871 through June 27, 1878 by James Innis (2007)

Cincinnati Enquirer Index (every name index 1934-1938) by Works Progress Administration (n.d.)

Cincinnati and Hamilton County, Ohio Post Office Letter Lists, 1794-1814; From Newspaper Files... by Marjorie Byrnside Burress (1982)

Pioneer Ohio Newspapers 1793-1810: Genealogical & Historical Abstracts (contains four Cincinnati area newspapers) by Karen Mauer Green (1986)

The Cincinnati Mirror and Ladies' Parterre, 1831-1833: Abstracts of Marriages, Obituaries, & Miscellanea by Paul Immel and Carol Montrose (2004)

Vital Statistics from the Cincinnati "Liberty Hall Gazette": Oct. 1863, Dec. 1863, Jan. 1-16, 1864 by Corinne M. Simons (1938)

Other publications

Columbia Township, Hamilton County, Ohio, Record Book: Selected Pages by General Reference Department of Public Library of Cincinnati and Hamilton County (1934)

Early Rosters of Cincinnati and Hamilton County by Marjorie Byrnside Burress (1984)

Hamilton County, Ohio Cemeteries: Names & Locations by Robert D. Craig (1963)

Hamilton County, Ohio, Citizenship Record Abstracts 1837-1916 by Lois E. Hughes (1991)

Hamilton County, Ohio Court and Other Records 3 Vol. by Virginia Raymond Cummins (1966)

Hamilton County, Ohio Naturalization and Marriage Records in the University of Cincinnati Archives by Kevin Grace (1987)

Index to Annual Reports of the Managers of the Widows' Home & Old Men's Home...1848-1961 (various years for deaths) by Chris Bell-Puckett (2001) CHLA

Index to Ohio Tax Lists, 1800-1810 Vol. 1 by Ronald Vern Jackson (1977)

Index to the Criminal Records in the Commissioners' Reports of the Court of Common Pleas of Hamilton County, Ohio for 1857-1865/1868-1871 by Chris Bell-Puckett (2002) CHLA

Marriage Records, 1808-1820, and Wills (Abstracts) 1790-1810 by Marie Dickoré (1959)

Ohio Military Land Warrants, 1789-1801 by Ronald Vern Jackson (1988)

Revolutionary Soldiers in Hamilton County, Ohio by Robert D. Craig (1965)

Revolutionary War Soldiers Buried in Hamilton County, Ohio by Historic Sites Committee, Cincinnati Chapter, Daughters of the American Revolution (2010)

Titus Atlas of Hamilton County, Ohio: From Actual Surveys (1869) by Clermont County Genealogical Society (1991)

Wills Filed in Probate Court, Hamilton County, Ohio, 1791-1901 by Lois E. Hughes (1991)

The Tracer Indexes, 1979–2018

Article indexes

The Tracer has published articles of exceptional instructional content and large lists of ancestral names relevant to Hamilton County. Indexes to all topics of *Tracer* articles through 2018 are on the HCGS website at https://hcgsohio.org/cpage.php?pt=109.

The articles listed in the index are characterized so readers can know instantly that the articles contain a list of possible ancestral names, or an explanation on how to do research on a particular topic, or where to access an online database, among other types. The article index can be printed or downloaded to a computer or cell phone to have on hand during research. All HCGS members have access to the *Tracer* issues with the articles from 2008 to the present on the HCGS website.

The articles are arranged in one or more categories. For example, information on veteran grave locations is under Military and/or the war of service and Cemetery.

African American	Irish
Bibliography	Jewish
Biography	Land & Leases at Hamilton Co. Recorder
Births - Ohio	Library Guides
Births & Adoptions - Local	Lineage Societies
Cemetery	Maps
Census, Directories & Voter lists	Marriage & Divorce
Church – Catholic	Military (See also Civil War)
Church – General and Other	Organizations, Lodges & Societies
Church - Protestant	Photographs
Cincinnati	Probate Court - Hamilton County
Civil War	Professions
Computers & Software	Research Guides
Courts and Law	Schools
Deaths and Burials - Local	Sources - Books and Journals
Deaths and Burials - Ohio	Sources - Miscellaneous
Events	Sources - Internet
France	Sources - Newspapers
Genetics & DNA	Taxes
Germany & Germans in Cincinnati (including Deutsche Pionier Verein indexes)	Towns and Townships (Hamilton Co. other than Cincinnati)
Ham. Co. Genealogical Society	War of 1812
Immigration and Naturalization	Women
Institutions, Hospitals, Asylums & Orphanages	World Wars I and II

Surname indexes

Cumulative and annual surname indexes contain all surnames published in a genealogical context for most years between 1979 and 2013. All surname indexes are on the Queries page, https://hcgsohio.org/cpage.php?pt=105.

Chapter 3: Religious Records and Resources

Cemeteries, Churches, and Funeral Home Records

Available at the Public Library of Cincinnati and Hamilton County and Norwood LDS on microfilm and where noted as digital versions online or through Family History Centers

RECORD NAME	LOCATION	DATES	LDS #	DIGITAL
CEMETERIES				
Baltimore Pike Cemetery	North Fairmount	1853 - 2008	2433305	8616907
Beech Grove Cemetery	Springfield Twp.	1889 - 1995	1994140	----
Bene Israel Congregation Mortuary Records		1895 - 1942	1012750	7948027
Bevis-Cedar Grove Cemetery	Colerain Twp.	1870 - 1930	1544104	----
Bridgetown Cemetery Association	Bridgetown		1535674	8616849
Calvary Cemetery	Duck Creek Rd.	1865 - 1992	1983603	----
Catherine St. Methodist Episcopal Cemetery	Catherine St.	1820 - 1866	1993163	8140337
Chestnut Street Cemetery (Jewish)	Chestnut St.		1012749	7951345
First German Protestant Cemetery	Vine St.	1843 - 1905	2156193	----
Hamilton County Cemetery Deeds		1859 - 1934	344600	7897630
Hoffner Cemetery	Mt. Healthy	1833 - 1919	1510065	8611440
Hopewell Cemetery Inscriptions	Montgomery		317453	7900611
Laurel Cemetery Deeds	Madisonville	1863 - 1949	893726	7902613
Mt. Washington Cemetery	Mt. Washington	1855 - 1957	1510035	8611433
Pleasant Ridge Presbyterian Cemetery	Pleasant Ridge	1800 - 1987	1509001	----
St. James Cemetery	White Oak	1937 - 1987	1514057	8611446
St. John Catholic Cemetery	St. Bernard	1849 - 1939	1510045	8140229
St. John Catholic Cemetery (Statistic Cards)	St. Bernard	1878 - 1987	1562211	4110926
St. Joseph New Cemetery (Irish) Vol. 1 - 17	Delhi Twp.	1868 - 1963	1510047	----
St. Joseph Old Cemetery - statistic sheets	Price Hill	1878 - 1987	1544067	8523737
St. Joseph Old Cemetery (German)	Price Hill	1845 - 1964	1514039	8188160
St. Joseph Old Cemetery (Irish part)	Price Hill	1850 - 1859	2026064	----
St. Mary Cemetery - burial records	St. Bernard	1877 - 1907	1514046	8140235
St. Mary Cemetery - statistic sheets	Ross Ave. St. Bernard	1878 - 1987	1544067	8523737
United Jewish Cemetery Association		1850 - 1951	978409	7989576
United Jewish Cemetery Association		1850 - 1959	899904	----
Vine Street Hill Cemetery (Single Burial records)	Vine St.	1851 - 1986	1510058	----
Vine Street Hill Cemetery (Statistics Cards)	Vine St.	1851 - 1986	1508981	----
Walnut Hills Cemetery (German Protestant)	Victory Parkway	1854 - 1939	1514049	8611441
Wesleyan Cemetery	Northside	1842 - 1994	1418410 1787552	----
CHURCHES				
Baptist				
Mt. Auburn Baptist	Auburn Ave.	1856 - 1985	1510041	8514469
Wyoming Baptist	Wyoming	1883 - 1936	1510054	8514473
Congregational				
Vine Street Congregational	Vine St.	1896 - 1900	2030565	8199859
Walnut Hills Congregational	Locust & Kemper Ln.	1843 - 1958	2030565	8199859

RECORD NAME	LOCATION	DATES	LDS #	DIGITAL
Episcopal				
Christ Church Cathedral	4th St.	1818 - 1982	1955202	8199109
Church of Our Savior	Mt. Auburn	1876 - 1986	1510048	----
Church of the Nativity	Grand Ave.	1880 - 1986	1510036	----
Church of the Resurrection	Sayler Park	1877 - 1998	2109601	8166767
Holy Trinity Episcopal		1882 - 1922	1510057	----
St. Luke Episcopal	Sayler Park	1877 - 1998	2109601	8166767
Evangelical (United Church of Christ)				
Camp Washington United Church of Christ	Camp Washington	1874 - 1979	1510053	8514472
Carthage United Church of Christ	Carthage	1871 - 1948	1514047	8514481
First German Reformed Church	Freeman Ave.	1844 - 1977	1902451	7856502
First United Church of Christ	Hoffner St.	1856 - 1983	1510056	7857130
Immanuel United Church of Christ	Queen City Ave.	1886 - 1986	1514071	8514486
Martini United Church of Christ	Lick Run	1852 - 1941	1510042	8198887
Matthew United Church of Christ	Winton Place	1911- 1957	1514054	8514482
Philippus United Church of Christ	McMicken & Ohio St.	1890 - 1953	1510063	----
Pilgrim United Church of Christ	Bridgetown Rd.	1871 - 1980	1862704	----
Salem United Church of Christ	Sycamore & Liberty	1856 - 1988	1548049	----
Salem Evangelical	Norwood	1911 - 1988	1763567	8515510
St. Jacob German Evangelical	West End	1881 - 1887	1686037	8166690
St. John Community - Northern Hills	Mt. Auburn	1874 - 1986	1510069	----
St. John Evangelical Church (Delhi)	Neeb Rd.	1864 - 1985	1510072	7769275
St. John Evangelical Lutheran Church	Sycamore Twp.	1873 - 1957	1535672	8140251
St. John Unitarian Church	12th & Elm Sts.	1839 - 1935	1510038	7857128
St. John United Church of Christ	Reading, OH	1879 - 1950	2108129	----
St. John United Church of Christ	Harrison, OH	1864 - 1952	1535673	8198878
St. Luke United Church of Christ	Glenmore Ave.	1865 - 1936	1514044	7857140
St. Mark German "Texas"	West End	1864 - 1930	1686041	7857500
St. Martin German Evangelical	River Rd.	1850 - 1964	1686036	7857499
St. Matthäus German Evangelical Reformed	Liberty & Elm Sts.	1843 - 1918	1514065	7857144
			1548046	7857187
St. Matthew United Church of Christ	Elmwood Place	1887 - 1954	1514117	----
St. Paul German Evangelical	15th & Race Sts.	1845 - 1948	1514059	7857142
			1535677	8332287
St. Paul United Church of Christ	Blue Rock Rd.	1856 - 1986	1510055	----
St. Peter German Evangelical	Main & McMicken	1842 - 1983	1514062	7769276
St. Peter Independent German Evangelical		1888 - 1901	1514072	8332285
St. Peter United Church of Christ	Ridge Rd.	1877 - 1953	1510071	8514476
Washington United Church of Christ	Camp Washington	1874 - 1979	1510053	8514472
Zion Evangelical Reformed	Norwood	1891 - 1978	1514055	8514483
Zion German Evangelical	15th & Bremen Sts.	1846 - 1934	1510057	----
Latter-day Saints (Mormon)				
Church of Jesus Christ of Latter-day Saints		1856 - 1861	0001968	----
Lutheran				
Church of Our Savior	Norwood	1902 - 1964	1514040	8514478
Concordia Lutheran	Race St.	1849 - 1953	1514042	8140234
Emmaus Lutheran	John & Bauer Sts.	1904 - 1927	1548050	8419558
First English Lutheran	Race St.	1841 - 1994	2030390	----

RECORD NAME	LOCATION	DATES	LDS #	DIGITAL
North German Lutheran Church	9th & Walnut Sts.	1814 - 1982	1763565	8140399
(Third Protestant Memorial)			1763571	7856966
St. Paul Lutheran	Madisonville	1866 - 1964	1514043	8198869
Third Protestant Memorial UCC	Ohio & Calhoun Sts.	1814 - 1982	1763565	8140399
(North German Lutheran)			1763571	7856966
Trinity Evangelical Lutheran	Mt. Healthy	1867 - 1923	1514070	----
Trinity Evangelical Lutheran	Race St.	1849 - 1924	1548050	8419558
Methodist				
Asbury Chapel Methodist Episcopal	Webster St.	1826 - 1936	1987642	8199801
Camp Washington Methodist Episcopal	Hopple St.	1889 - 1958	2020900	8140342
Carthage Methodist Church	Carthage	1876 - 1969	2312944	----
Christie Chapel	Catherine St.	1851 - 1908	2020899	8199844
Clifton Methodist Episcopal Church	Clifton	1891 - 1930	1510070	8514475
East Pearl St. Methodist Episcopal	E. Pearl St.	1855 - 1929	1987642	8199801
Ebenezer Circuit Methodist Episcopal	Bridgetown Rd.	1845 - 1848	2020899	8199844
Epworth United Methodist	Mt. Healthy	1852 - 1925	1514041	8514479
Faith Methodist	Elmwood Place	1969 - 1989	2312944	----
Finley Chapel Methodist Episcopal	Clinton St.	1897 - 1930	2020899	8199844
Harrison United Methodist	Harrison, OH	1855 - 1986	1510043	8514470
Heritage United Methodist	Mt. Healthy	1833 - 1919	1510065	8611440
Mears Chapel Methodist Episcopal	Plum St.	1865 - 1873	2020899	8199844
Methodist Episcopal Preacher's Relief Society		1839 - 1925	2021132	----
Miami Circuit Methodist Episcopal		1834 - 1870	2020900	8140342
Montgomery & Bethel Methodist Episcopal	Montgomery	1885 - 1928	2020900	8140342
Morris Chapel Methodist Episcopal	Central Ave.	1864 - 1875	2020897	8516326
Nast-Trinity United Methodist	Race St.	1835 - 1985	2027239	8516343
Spring Grove German Methodist Episcopal	Spring Grove Ave.	1909 - 1934	2020900	8140342
St. Paul Methodist Episcopal	7th & Smith Sts.	1864 - 1875	2020897	8516326
Third German Methodist Episcopal		1826 - 1936	1987642	8199801
Trinity Methodist Episcopal	9th St.	1950 - 1958	2027239	8516343
Union Chapel Methodist Episcopal	7th St.	1854 - 1945	2020899	8199844
Walnut Hills - Avondale United Methodist		1865 - 1970	2057382	8166749
Wesley Chapel Methodist Episcopal	5th St.	1834 - 1985	1987642	8199801
West Chester Circuit Methodist Episcopal		1834 - 1870	2020900	8140342
Winton Place Methodist Episcopal	Winton Place	1866 - 1971	2021131	8516328
York St. Methodist Episcopal	Baymiller & York	1859 - 1945	2020898	8516327
Presbyterian				
Avondale Presbyterian	Reading Rd.	1867 - 1948	2026509	8516337
Central & Covenant Presbyterian		1844 - 1907	1954691	8515403
Central Presbyterian	5th St.	1844 - 1907	1954691	8515403
Church of the Covenant		1901 - 1964	1954949	8515400
Elberon Presbyterian	Rapid Run Pk.	1914 - 1941	2031014	----
Fifth Presbyterian	5th & Elm Sts.	1833 - 1909	1954690	8199115
First German Presbyterian	Linn St.	1855 - 1918	2048136	8518156
First Presbyterian	4th St.	1811 - 1960	1954950	7842538
First Presbyterian - Delhi	Delhi Twp.	1832 - 1905	1686037	8166690
First Presbyterian - Walnut Hills	Gilbert Ave.	1819 - 1994	2026508	8516336
First Reformed Presbyterian	Plum St.	1854 - 1914	1954690	8199115
First United Presbyterian		1841 - 1881	914075	8510094

RECORD NAME	LOCATION	DATES	LDS #	DIGITAL
Lane Seminary - Presbyterian	Walnut Hills	1831 - 1878	2030565	8199859
Lincoln Park Presbyterian		1870 - 1871	1955127	8140328
Montgomery Presbyterian	Montgomery	1820 - 1932	1510044	7857129
North Presbyterian		1855 - 1928	1514058	8514484
Norwood Presbyterian	Norwood	1886 - 1911	1510037	8514467
Pleasant Ridge Presbyterian	Pleasant Ridge	1814 - 1925	0859778	7712477
			1514038	8198870
Presbyterian Church in Cincinnati	Historical Record	1811 - 1964	1954690	8199115
Reformed Presbyterian			1954950	7842538
Second German Presbyterian	Liberty St.	1857 - 1930	1954690	8199115
Second Presbyterian	4th St.	1816 - 1916	1955128	8140329
Third Presbyterian		1836 - 1860	525750	7548749
Trinity Presbyterian		1945 - 1961	2031014	----
Walnut Hills United Presbyterian	Walnut Hills	1941 - 1994	2026509	8516337
West Cincinnati Presbyterian	Linn St. & Poplar St.	1859 - 1959	1510066	8166675
			2048136	8518156
West Liberty Presbyterian		1867 - 1930	1954950	7842538
Westminster Presbyterian	Price Hill	1883 - 1956	1510067	8166676
Wyoming Presbyterian	Wyoming	1870 - 1924	1510068	----
Society of Friends (Quaker)				
Society of Friends Meeting Minutes		1762 - 1896	364703	8132975
Society of Friends Meeting Minutes - Orthodox	Poplar St.	1754 - 1961	974060	----
United Brethren				
Hoffner Memorial United Brethren		1833 - 1919	1544170	8142207
Willey Memorial United Brethren		1951 - 1967	2020898	8516327
Miscellaneous				
Goodwill Church		1941 - 1943	2027239	8516343
Heritage Unitarian Church		1887 - 1969	1510040	8514468
Maley, Rev George (marriages)		1851 - 1852	2021131	8516328
Montgomery Universalist	Montgomery	1839 - 1943	1514045	8514480
New Jerusalem		1811 - 1971	1630318	8515470
Societies and Churches – incorporation records		1847 - 1919	344602	----

FUNERAL HOMES

RECORD NAME	LOCATION	DATES	LDS #	DIGITAL
Barrere Funeral Home	Eastern Ave.	1927 - 1953	1698293	----
Fuldner Funeral Home	Sycamore St.	1866 - 1936	1535657	4031463
Gerhardt Funeral Home		1853 - 1879	1535676	7712631
Hawthorne Funeral Home	Mt. Healthy	1914 - 1967	1514048	4030354
Hodapp Funeral Home		1903 - 1954	1510059	4030271
Neidhard Minges Funeral Home		1868 - 1950	1535666	8574349
Radel Funeral Home	Lower Price Hill	1909 - 1932	1487711	----
Rebold Funeral Home (Vol. 1 - 16)	Queen City Ave.	1897 - 1949	1535668	7579802
Seward Funeral Home		1887 - 1899	1535676	7712631
T.P. White & Sons Funeral Home	Mt. Washington	1936 - 1976	2108388	----
Vitt and Stermer Funeral Home (Vol. 1 - 38)	Westwood Ave.	1899 - 1934	1514066	----
Weil Funeral Home (Jewish)		1913 - 2015	HCGS website	
Wiltsee / Schaeffer & Busby Funeral Home		1855 - 1968	1983603	----
Wiltsee Funeral Home (Vol. 1 - 46)	W. 6th St.	1852 - 1937	1535654	4030356

FamilySearch is continually working to scan and digitize more microfilm rolls and migrate to a digital format. Some of these digital copies may be viewed from home and some may require the researcher to be at a Family History Center library for viewing. Most of these records are on more than one roll of microfilm. Only the first microfilm number has been listed here. Consult the FamilySearch catalog to view a complete listing for each record. See page 87 for further information on viewing digitized microfilm.

For more details and links to indexes of religious records, see these pages on the HCGS website, https://hcgsohio.org: Religious Records, Religious Institutions, Baptisms and Birth Records, Death Records, Marriages and Divorces. An exhaustive reference on 573 local institutions is available as a PDF linked from the Religious Institutions web page.

Records of the Archdiocese of Cincinnati

In early 2019 some of the sacramental records for the nineteen counties of the Archdiocese of Cincinnati were digitized and made available online through Findmypast, a subscription website, at https://www.findmypast.com. There are various options for researchers to search and view records.

Researchers may also request copies of specific records and limited research services directly from the Archives of the Archdiocese of Cincinnati. Download a request form, print and complete it, and mail it to Archdiocese of Cincinnati Archives, 100 E. 8th Street, Cincinnati, OH 45202.

Alternatively, fill out the form online and submit a request along with payment using a credit card electronically. For information on how to request research services and updated information to obtain copies, consult the website at http://www.catholiccincinnati.org/ministries-offices/archives-office/genealogy.

For more information about the history of the Archdiocese of Cincinnati and access to digitized histories, visit these websites compiled by the Archdiocese Archives:

- http://www.catholiccincinnati.org/about-us-2/a-protrait
- http://www.catholiccincinnati.org/ministries-offices/archives-office/digitized-histories

Tracer articles, December 2015:

- "Locating and Requesting Catholic Records in the Archdiocese of Cincinnati"
- "Tracing Your Cincinnati Catholic Ancestors"
- "Hamilton County Marriage Banns, 1883-1949"

Cincinnati Catholic Newspapers

- *American Catholic Tribune*, 1886-1894, the first African American Catholic newspaper in the United States. Issues at PLCH.
- *Catholic Telegraph*, 1831-to date, the official weekly newspaper of the Archdiocese of Cincinnati, and the oldest continuing Catholic newspaper in the U.S. On microfilm at PLCH, digitized in Digital Library.
- *Volksfreund*, 1850-1908, read primarily by German Catholics; indexed by Jeffrey Herbert in *Index of Death Notices and Marriage Notices Appearing in the* Cincinnati Volksfreund, *1850-1908,* and the public HCGS Death Notice Index, http://hcgsohio.org/cpage.php?pt=62#Public. Issues on microfilm at PLCH. 1863-1904 images on GenealogyBank (subscription site).
- *Wahrheitsfreund*, 1837-1908, the first German Catholic newspaper in the U.S. Issues on microfilm at PLCH and the University of Cincinnati's Archives and Rare Books Library, selected issues online at HathiTrust (https://catalog.hathitrust.org/Record/012100358).

Roman Catholic Churches in Hamilton County, 1818–1921

Organized	Name of Church	Location	Year Records Begin			19th Century
			Baptisms	Marriages	Burials	Ethnicity
1818	St. Peter in Chains Cathedral (original name Christ Church)	8th & Plum	1839	1839	1839-49 1903 -	Irish
1834	Holy Trinity	5th & Mound	1834	1834	1834	German - closed
1840	St. James the Greater	White Oak	1844	1846	1880	
1840	Old St. Mary	13th & Main	1842	1842	1842	German
1842	Our Lady of Victory	Delhi Twp.	1844	1855	1854	German
1844	St. John the Baptist	Green & Republic	1845	1845	1846	German - closed
1844	St. Peter	Lick Run	1854	1854	1854	German - closed
1845	St. Francis Xavier	Sycamore St.	1845	1846	1891	Irish
1845	All Saints	E. 3rd St.	1850	1851	1926	Irish - closed
1846	St. Philomena	3rd & Pearl	1848	1848	1848	German - closed
1846	St. Joseph	Ezzard Charles Dr.	1847	1847	1847	German
1847	St. Michael the Archangel	St. Michael St.	1848	1848	1848	German - closed
1848	St. Paul	12th & Spring	1850	1850	1850	German - closed
1849	St. Francis de Sales	Woodburn	1850	1851	1909	German
1850	St. Patrick	3rd & Mill	1850	1851	none	Irish - closed
1850	St. Clement	St. Bernard, OH	1850	1850	1851	
1850	Sts. Peter and Paul	Reading, OH	1851	1851	1869	German
1850	St. John the Baptist	Harrison, OH	1850	1853	1857	
1852	St. Augustine	Bank St.	1853	1853	1857	German - closed
1852	St. Willibord	Liberty & Walnut	No surviving records			Dutch - closed
1853	St. Jerome	California	1863	1863	1912	
1853	St. Patrick	Northside	1853	1854	1922	Irish - closed
1854	St. Thomas	5th & Sycamore	1853	1853	none	Irish - closed
1854	Assumption	Mt. Healthy	1860	1864	1866	
1857	St. Gabriel	Glendale, OH	1862	1862	1873	Irish
1858	St. Anthony	Madisonville	1859	1863	1867	
1858	St. Francis Seraph	Liberty & Vine	1859	1860	1860	German
1859	Immaculata	Mt. Adams	1860	1863	1863	German
1859	Holy Angels	Grandin Rd.	1859	1860	1885	Irish - closed
1860	St. Anthony	Budd St.	1860	1860	1860	German - closed
1860	St. John the Baptist	Dry Ridge	1863	1864	1864	
1860	St. Joseph	North Bend, OH	prior to 1914 records at St. Aloysius on the Ohio			
1861	St. Vincent de Paul	Sedamsville	1862	1863	1862	Irish
1862	St. Boniface	Northside	1862	1863	1895	German
1864	St. Edward	Clark & Mound	1864	1864	1918	Irish - closed
1866	St. Aloysius Gonzaga	Bridgetown	1868	1868	1868	
1866	St. Ann	Richmond & Court	1866	1867	1909	African-American
1867	St. Bernard	Taylor Creek	1871	1903	1888	
1867	St. Rose of Lima	Riverside Dr.	1868	1868	1881	German
1867	St. Stephen	Columbia-Tusculum	1867	1869	1893	
1868	St. Aloysius on the Ohio	Sayler Park	1873	1873	1876	

Organized	Name of Church	Location	Baptisms	Marriages	Burials	Ethnicity
1868	St. Bonaventure	South Fairmount	1869	1869	1870	German - closed
1868	St. George	Corryville	1868	1869	1871	German - closed
1868	St. Lawrence O'Toole	Price Hill	1856	1870	1868	German
1869	St. Charles Borromeo	Carthage	1869	1870	1880	closed
1870	Atonement	3rd St.	1872	1873	1873	closed
1870	Sacred Heart of Jesus	Camp Washington	1870	1871	1870	German
1870	St. Louis (St. Ludwig)	8th & Walnut	1870	1870	1871	German
1871	Assumption	Walnut Hills	1872	1873	1878	
1873	Holy Cross	Mt. Adams	1873	1873	1873	Irish - closed
1873	St. Henry	Flint St.	1873	1874	1934	German - closed
1873	St. Stanislaus	Liberty & Cutter	1875	1875	none	Polish
1874	St. Andrew	Avondale	1875	1878	1879	Irish
1874	Blessed Sacrament	Lower Price Hill	1874	1875	1912	Irish - closed
1874	Our Lady of the Sacred Heart	Reading, OH	1879	1879	1879	German
1878	Our Lady of Perpetual Help	Sedamsville	1878	1878	1878	German - closed
1883	Holy Family	Price Hill	1884	1885	1884	
1884	St. Elizabeth	Norwood	1886	1887	1886	merged
1886	St. Leo the Great	North Fairmount	1886	1901	1901	
1887	St. Aloysius	Elmwood Place	1889	1889	1890	closed
1887	St. James in the Valley	Wyoming	1887	1887	1888	
1890	Sacred Heart	Camp Washington	1890	1890	1893	Italian
1891	St. John the Evangelist	Deer Park	1892	1895	1906	
1892	St. Agnes	Bond Hill	1892	1895	1893	
1892	Guardian Angels	Mt. Washington	1892	1893	1895	
1898	St. Mary	Hyde Park	1901	1901	1905	
1902	St. Catharine	Westwood	1903	1903	1904	
1903	Our Lady of Loretto	East End	1904	1904	1904	closed
1904	Holy Name	Auburn Ave.	1905	1905	1905	
1904	St. Mark	Evanston	1905	1905	1906	closed
1906	St. Matthew	Norwood	1907	1907	1907	merged
1906	St. Peter & Paul	Norwood	1906	1906	1906	merged
1908	St. Cecilia	Oakley	1908	1909	1909	
1909	St. Clare	College Hill	1909	1910	1909	
1909	St. William	Price Hill	1910	1910	1910	
1910	Annunciation	Clifton	1910	1910	1910	
1910	St. Anthony of Padua	Walnut Hills	1911	1911	1911	Marionite
1910	St. Monica	Clifton Heights	1911	1911	1911	
1910	St. Pius	Cumminsville	1911	1911	1911	
1911	St. Martin of Tours	Cheviot	1911	1911	1911	
1914	St. Joseph of Nazareth	Liberty & Elm	1919	1919	1919	Hungarian - closed
1915	Holy Spirit Chapel	Downtown	1916	1915	1924	closed
1916	St. Teresa of Avila	Price Hill	1916	1917	1916	
1917	Nativity of Our Lord	Pleasant Ridge	1917	1917	1917	
1919	Resurrection of Our Lord	Price Hill	1919	1919	1919	
1919	St. Bernard	Winton Place	1919	1919	1919	
1919	St. Michael	Sharonville	1919	1920	1919	
1920	St. Margaret Mary	North College Hill	1920	1920	1921	
1921	St. Margaret of Cortona	Madisonville	1920	1922	1920	

There are many newer Roman Catholic churches.

Genealogy of Some Roman Catholic Churches
in Cincinnati and Hamilton County, 1822–1992

The charts below are taken from pages 328 and 329 of the *History of the Archdiocese of Cincinnati 1821–1921* by Rev. John H. Lamott, STD, published in 1921 by Frederick Pustet Company, Inc.

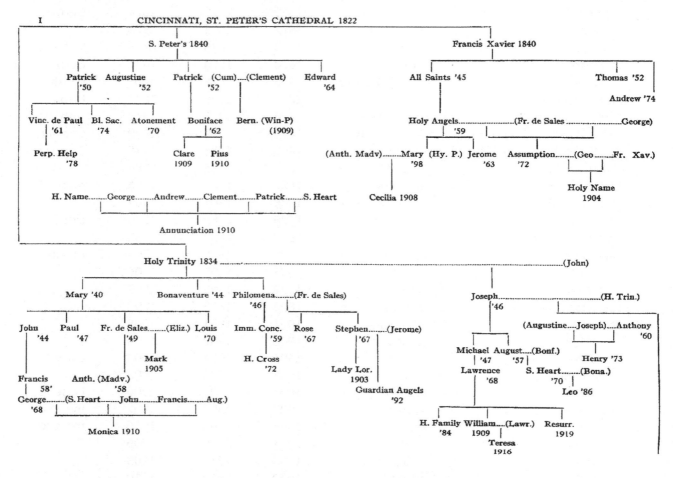

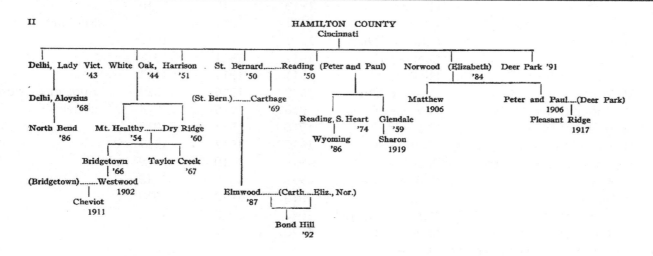

Genealogy of Some German Lutheran Churches in Cincinnati, 1849–1986

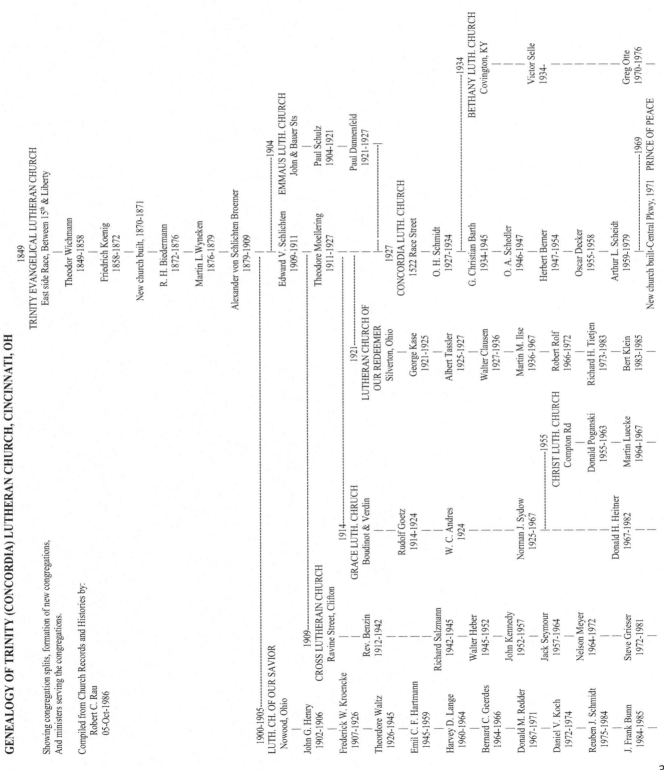

GENEALOGY OF TRINITY (CONCORDIA) LUTHERAN CHURCH, CINCINNATI, OH

Showing congregation splits, formation of new congregations,
And ministers serving the congregations.

Compiled from Church Records and Histories by:
Robert C. Rau
05-Oct-1986

1849
TRINITY EVANGELICAL LUTHERAN CHURCH
East side Race, Between 15th & Liberty

Theodor Wichmann 1849-1858
Friedrich Koenig 1858-1872
New church built, 1870-1871
R. H. Biedermann 1872-1876
Martin L. Wyneken 1876-1879
Alexander von Schlichten Broemer 1879-1909

1904
EMMAUS LUTH. CHURCH
John & Bauer Sts

Edward V. Schlichten 1909-1911
Theodore Moellering 1911-1927
Paul Schulz 1904-1921
Paul Dannenfeld 1921-1927

1927
CONCORDIA LUTH. CHURCH
1522 Race Street

O. H. Schmidt 1927-1934
G. Christian Barth 1934-1945
O. A. Schedler 1946-1947
Herbert Berner 1947-1954
Oscar Decker 1955-1958
Arthur L. Scheidt 1959-1979

1934
BETHANY LUTH. CHURCH
Covington, KY

Victor Selle 1934-

Greg Otte 1970-1976
PRINCE OF PEACE

New church built-Central Pkwy, 1971

1921
LUTHERAN CHURCH OF
OUR REDEEMER
Silverton, Ohio

George Kase 1921-1925
Albert Tassler 1925-1927
Walter Clausen 1927-1936
Martin M. Ilse 1936-1967
Robert Rolf 1966-1972
Richard H. Tietjen 1973-1983
Bert Klein 1983-1985

1914
GRACE LUTH. CHRUCH
Boudinot & Verdin

Rudolf Goetz 1914-1924
W. C. Andres 1924
Norman J. Sydow 1925-1967

1955
CHRIST LUTH. CHURCH
Compton Rd

Donald Poganski 1955-1963
Martin Luecke 1964-1967
Donald H. Heitner 1967-1982

1900-1905
LUTH. CH. OF OUR SAVIOR
Nowood, Ohio

John G. Henry 1902-1906

1909
CROSS LUTHERAIN CHURCH
Ravine Street, Clifton

Frederick W. Kroencke 1907-1926
Rev. Benzin 1912-1942
Richard Salzmann 1942-1945
Walter Heber 1945-1952
John Kennedy 1952-1957
Jack Seymour 1957-1964

Emil C. F. Hartmann 1945-1959
Harvey D. Lange 1960-1964
Bernard C. Geerdes 1964-1966
Donald M. Redder 1967-1971
Daniel V. Koch 1972-1974
Nelson Meyer 1964-1972
Reuben J. Schmidt 1975-1984
Steve Grieser 1972-1981
J. Frank Bunn 1984-1985

31

Genealogy of Some German Evangelical Churches in Cincinnati, 1810–1992

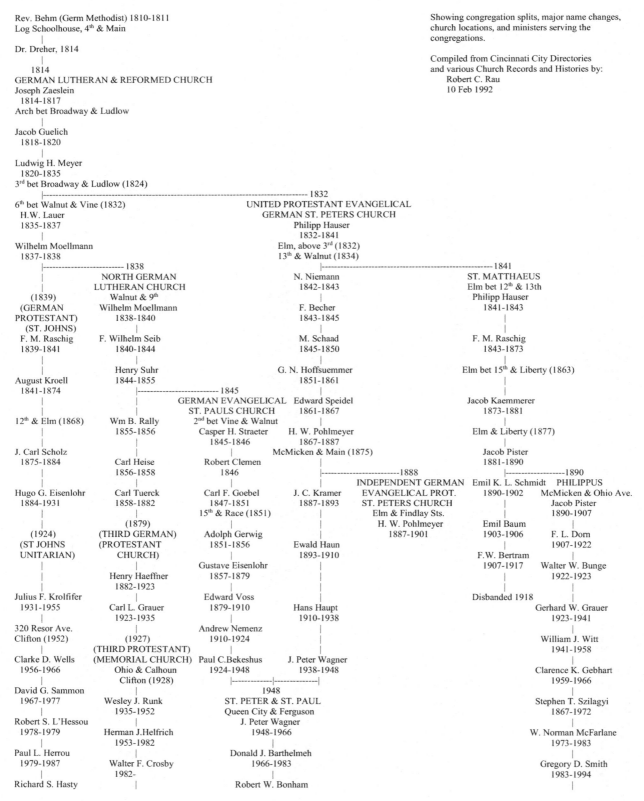

Rev. Behm (Germ Methodist) 1810-1811
Log Schoolhouse, 4th & Main
|
Dr. Dreher, 1814
|
1814
GERMAN LUTHERAN & REFORMED CHURCH
Joseph Zaeslein
1814-1817
Arch bet Broadway & Ludlow
|
Jacob Guelich
1818-1820
|
Ludwig H. Meyer
1820-1835
3rd bet Broadway & Ludlow (1824)
|--- 1832
6th bet Walnut & Vine (1832)   UNITED PROTESTANT EVANGELICAL
H.W. Lauer   GERMAN ST. PETERS CHURCH
1835-1837   Philipp Hauser
| 1832-1841
Wilhelm Moellmann   Elm, above 3rd (1832)
1837-1838   13th & Walnut (1834)
|------------------------ 1838 |-- 1841
NORTH GERMAN   N. Niemann   ST. MATTHAEUS
LUTHERAN CHURCH   1842-1843   Elm bet 12th & 13th
(1839)   Walnut & 9th | Philipp Hauser
(GERMAN   Wilhelm Moellmann   F. Becher   1841-1843
PROTESTANT)   1838-1840   1843-1845 |
(ST. JOHNS) | | F. M. Raschig
F. M. Raschig   F. Wilhelm Seib   M. Schaad   1843-1873
1839-1841   1840-1844   1845-1850
| Henry Suhr   G. N. Hoffsuemmer   Elm bet 15th & Liberty (1863)
August Kroell   1844-1855   1851-1861 |
1841-1874 |------------------------ 1845   Jacob Kaemmerer
| | GERMAN EVANGELICAL Edward Speidel 1873-1881
12th & Elm (1868)   Wm B. Rally   ST. PAULS CHURCH   1861-1867 |
| 1855-1856   2nd bet Vine & Walnut | Elm & Liberty (1877)
J. Carl Scholz | Casper H. Straeter   H. W. Pohlmeyer |
1875-1884   Carl Heise   1845-1846   1867-1887   Jacob Pister
| 1856-1858 | McMicken & Main (1875) 1881-1890
Hugo G. Eisenlohr   Carl Tuerck   Robert Clemen |------------------------1888   Emil K. L. Schmidt   PHILIPPUS
1884-1931   1858-1882   1846   INDEPENDENT GERMAN   1890-1902   McMicken & Ohio Ave.
| | Carl F. Goebel J. C. Kramer EVANGELICAL PROT. | Jacob Pister
| (1879)   1847-1851   1887-1893 ST. PETERS CHURCH Emil Baum   1890-1907
(1924)   (THIRD GERMAN) 15th & Race (1851) Elm & Findlay Sts. 1903-1906 |
(ST JOHNS   (PROTESTANT) | | H. W. Pohlmeyer | F. L. Dorn
UNITARIAN)   CHURCH)   Adolph Gerwig   Ewald Haun   1887-1901 F.W. Bertram 1907-1922
| | 1851-1856   1893-1910 | 1907-1917 |
Julius F. Krolfifer Henry Haeffner Gustave Eisenlohr | | Walter W. Bunge
1931-1955   1882-1923   1857-1879 | Disbanded 1918 1922-1923
| | Edward Voss   Hans Haupt |
320 Resor Ave.   Carl L. Grauer 1879-1910   1910-1938   Gerhard W. Grauer
Clifton (1952)   1923-1935   Andrew Nemenz   1923-1941
| (1927)   1910-1924 |
Clarke D. Wells   (THIRD PROTESTANT) | William J. Witt
1956-1966   (MEMORIAL CHURCH) Paul C.Bekeshus J. Peter Wagner   1941-1958
| Ohio & Calhoun 1924-1948   1938-1948 |
David G. Sammon   Clifton (1928) |-------------|-------------| Clarence K. Gebhart
1967-1977 | 1948   1959-1966
| Wesley J. Runk ST. PETER & ST. PAUL |
Robert S. L'Hessou   1935-1952   Queen City & Ferguson   Stephen T. Szilagyi
1978-1979 | J. Peter Wagner   1867-1972
| Herman J.Helfrich 1948-1966 |
Paul L. Herrou   1953-1982 | W. Norman McFarlane
1979-1987 | Donald J. Barthelmeh   1973-1983
| Walter F. Crosby 1966-1983 |
Richard S. Hasty   1982- | Gregory D. Smith
| Robert W. Bonham   1983-1994
                                                                              |

Showing congregation splits, major name changes, church locations, and ministers serving the congregations.

Compiled from Cincinnati City Directories and various Church Records and Histories by:
Robert C. Rau
10 Feb 1992

Episcopal Churches in Hamilton County, 1817–1997

Organized	Name of Church	Location	Notes
1817	Christ Church	4th St	
1834	St. Paul	4th St	closed
1841	Grace Church	Cincinnati	mission of St. Paul
1843	Trinity	Liberty St.	closed
1849	St. John	7th & Plum Sts.	closed
1855	Church of the Advent	Walnut Hills	
1856	Calvary	Clifton	
1857	Church of the Redemption	Downtown (northeast)	
1858	Church of the Atonement	Riverside	
1863	St. James	Richmond St.	(merger of Redemption & Atonement) closed
1865	Christ Church	Glendale, OH	
1866	Grace Church	Avondale	
1872	Emmanuel	Cincinnati	
1872	St. Philip	Cumminsville	
1875	St. Luke	Downtown	
1876	Church of Our Savior	Mt. Auburn	
1877	St. Thomas	Terrace Park	(original address Montauk)
1877	Church of the Resurrection	Fernbank	now called St. Luke (Sayler Park)
1879	Church of the Nativity	Price Hill	
1880	Holy Trinity	Hartwell	
1880	Epiphany	Walnut Hills?	
1880	St. Mark	Oakley	
1884	Holy Trinity	Madisonville	
1885	St. Stephen	Winton Place	
1890	Church of the Good Shepherd	Norwood	
1893	Church of the Ascension	Wyoming	
1895	St. Andrew	Cincinnati	mission of St. Luke, Addyston
1897	St. Peter	Carthage	
1908	Church of the Redeemer	Hyde Park	
1917	All Saints	Pleasant Ridge	
1922	St. James	Westwood	
1931	Indian Hill Church	Indian Hill	(Episcopal & Presbyterian)
1933	St. Matthew	Bond Hill	
1933	St. Simon of Cyrene	Woodlawn Terrace	(later Lincoln Heights)
1956	Church of the Holy Spirit	Forest Park	
1956	St. Timothy	Mount Washington	
1981	St. Barnabas	Montgomery	

Records from the closed churches are located at the Episcopal Archives (closed to the public):
Episcopal Diocese of Southern Ohio
412 Sycamore St.
Cincinnati, OH 45202
(513) 421-0311

More information about the history of the Episcopal Diocese of Cincinnati:
https://cincinnaticathedral.com/about-history
A Centennial History of Christ Church, Cincinnati, 1817-1917, by Wm. H. Venable (1918)

Jewish Congregations in Hamilton County, 1824–2016

1824-	KK Bene Israel (Rockdale Temple)
1839-	KK Bene Yesherun (Wise Temple)
1850-1906	Ahebeth Achim (Society of Brotherly Love) - 1906: merged KK Sherith Israel
1851-1852	Holy Congregation Gates of Heaven - 1852: split: Bene Israel / Adath Israel
1853-	Adath Israel (Polish shul)
1855-1931	KK Sherith Israel - 1931: merged Wise Temple
1869-1959	KK Beth Tefila (Lithuanian shul)
1880-1900	KK Beth Hamedrash
1882-	Ohav Shalom (Russian shul) - 2014 = Etz Chaim
1883-1899	Hevra Beth Hakenisis - split from Beth Tefila
1886-1979	Beth Hamedrash Hagedol (Bond Hill Synagogue)
1888-1890	Wohafte Fredo Jewish Church
1894-1935	Anshe Polen -1935: merged Beth Hamedrash Hagedol
1895-1998	Yad Charuzim (Austrian-Hungarian - North Avondale)
1898-1908	Anshe Chesed
1902-1924	Agudath Achim 1924: merged Bnai Israel = Anshei Sholom
1910-1946	Tifereth Israel - 1946: merged Yad Charuzim = North Avondale Synagogue
1912-	Kneseth Israel (Washington Ave Synagogue) - 2008 = Zichron Eliezer
1914-1967	Bnai Avraham - 1967: merged Northern Hills
1917-1924	Bnai (Bene) Israel (Romanian shul) - 1924: merged Agudath Achim = Anshei Sholom
1922-1970	Beth Jacob
1923-1949	Tifereth Zion (Avondale branch of Ohav Shalom)
1923-	Bnai Jacob (Polish shul = Agudas Israel = Golf Manor) - 1957= Golf Manor
1924-1933	Anshei Sholom - 1933: merged Bnai Jacob = Agudas Israel
1933-1993	Beth Sholom (Sefardic)
1936-1999?	Kheleth Bnei Israel (Carmels shul) - split from Beth Hamedrash Hagedol
1939-1999	Tikvoh Chodoshoh (German shul = New Hope)
1945-2004	Downtown Synagogue (Vaad Synagogue)
1948-2006	Agudath Achim (Roselawn Synagogue)
1954-	Temple Sholom
1959-	Valley Temple
1960-	Northern Hills Synagogue (Bnai Avraham)
1964-2014	Bnai Tzedek - 2014: merged Ohav Shalom = Etz Chaim
1980-	Beth Adam
1998-2011	Bnai Tikvah
2004-2007	Beit Chaverim - 2007: merged Bnai Tzedek
2011-	Sha'arei Torah (Village Schul)

A more thorough exploration of Jewish congregations in Hamilton County can be found on the HCGS website at https://hcgsohio.org/cpage.php?pt=163.

Jewish Resources

General resources

JewishGen (https://www.jewishgen.org). The top site for Jewish genealogical research, powered by Ancestry and supported by donations. Access to databases and special interest groups. Self-paced online courses available.

Jewish Records Indexing—Poland (https://jri-poland.org). Similar to JewishGen, but focused on Poland. Shares some content with JewishGen. A must for anyone with Polish heritage.

Routes to Roots Foundation (http://rtrfoundation.org/index.shtml). Most complete online directory of Jewish records of genealogical interest. Covers Belarus, Lithuania, Moldova, Poland and Ukraine.

Yad Vashem, the World Holocaust Remembrance Center (http://yvng.yadvashem.org). Maintains central database of Shoah victims' names. Pages of testimony often include extended family details.

Avotaynu (http://avotaynu.com). Extensive online catalog of periodicals and books related to Jewish genealogical research.

International Association of Jewish Genealogical Societies (http://www.iajgs.org). Hosts an annual convention.

One-Step Webpages by Steven P. Morse (https://stevemorse.org). Specialized search portals and other tools for many online resources (census, passenger records, vital records, Holocaust research) and outstanding conversion tools for calendars (Jewish, Julian, Gregorian) and character sets (including Hebrew and Cyrillic print and script).

Blood and Frogs: Jewish Genealogy and More (https://bloodandfrogs.com/compendium). Links to 25,000 resources. Like Cyndi's List, only strictly Jewish.

Local resources

American Israelite (https://www.americanisraelite.com), America's oldest English-language Jewish newspaper.

Jewish Cemeteries of Greater Cincinnati (https://www.jcemcin.org). Cemeteries index with photos.

Weil Funeral Home. The oldest and nearly the only Jewish funeral home serving the Greater Cincinnati region since about 1912. Digitized copies of the Weil burial index cards are accessible to HCGS members via the website.

Hebrew Union College's Klau Library (http://huc.edu/research/libraries/cincinnati-klau-library) and the American Jewish Archives (http://www.americanjewisharchives.org). Access to out-of-town Jewish newspapers, both online and print, family genealogies, temple bulletins, congregation records, rabbis' papers, and free access to the American Israelite Online Archives.

Books

Fine, John S. and Frederic J. Krome. *Jews of Cincinnati*. Charleston, SC: Arcadia Publishers, 2007.

Mokotoff, Gary. *Getting Started in Jewish Genealogy*. New Haven, CT: Avotaynu, 2018.

Segal, Joshua L. *A Field Guide to Visiting a Jewish Cemetery*. Nashua, NH: Jewish Cemetery Publishing, 2005.

Articles

HCGS Jewish Interest Group articles, *The Tracer*, June 2015 – June 2018

"Genealogical Resources at the American Jewish Archives," *The Tracer,* February 2007

Chapter 4: Court and Land Records

Hamilton County Probate Court

William Howard Taft Center (WHTC)

230 East Ninth St. (Sycamore & Ninth Sts.)

Cincinnati, OH 45202

(513) 946-3551

M-F: 8-4 p.m., 9th Floor Historical Records

www.probatect.org > Court Records > Archive Search

COLLECTION	DATES	FORMAT	PLACE
Estate & Guardianship Dockets vol. 1 to 4, arranged by case #	1791 – 1847	Scanned images from original books	www.probatect.org*,#
Estate, Trust & Guardianship Dockets & cases, vol. 1-440	1852 – 1984	Scanned images from original books	"
Probate Court Journal Entries, vol. 1-4, each vol. indexed	1791 – 1837	Scanned images from original books	www.probatect.org**,#
Will Index Books, 1 to 39	1791 – 1884	Scanned images	www.probatect.org*,#
Will vol. 40 - 561, each vol. indexed	1791 – 1973	from original books	
Marriage License and Record Indexes, vol. 1-109	1817 – 1983	Scanned images from original books	www.probatect.org°#
Marriage Banns, vol. 1-20 (Catholic)	1883 – 1953	" "	"
Marriage Record, vol. A1-29	1808 – 1875	" "	"
Marriage Record, vol. B1-30	1952 – 1888	" "	"
Marriage Record vol. 22 to 89	1859 – 1880	" "	"
Marriage Licenses, vol. 92-370	1859, 1885 –	" "	"
Marriage Record, vol. C1-10	1928	Only on microfilm	(WHTC 9th floor)
Marriage Record, vol. C12-139	1884 restored	Only on microfilm	(WHTC 9th floor)
Marriage Licenses, vol. 91	1884 – 1931	Films MLB-1 to 156	
Marriage Licenses, vol. 371-818	1928 – 1973	Only on microfiche	(WHTC 9th floor)
Marriage Licenses	1973 – 1984	Searchable index	(WHTC 9th floor)
Marriage Licenses	1984 – present	Only on microfilm	www.probatect.org
Marriage License consents vol. 1-8	1973 – 1976		(WHTC 9th floor)
Minister's License	1840 – 1976	Only on microfilm	(WHTC 9th floor)
Minister's License Index	1963 – 1975	Scanned images from original books	www.probatect.org
Birth Index & Records, 2 vols. (very incomplete)	1863 – 1908	Scanned images from original books	www.probatect.org**,#
Birth Registration & Correction,			"
vol. 1 - 9, with index	1941 – 1965	" "	
vol. 10, 11, with index	1966 – 1994	" "	

COLLECTION	DATES	FORMAT	PLACE
Birth Correction Journal Entries, vol. 53, 54	1968 – 1974	" "	"
Death Records, no master index, vol. 1 - 4 (very incomplete)	1881 – 1908	Scanned images from original books	www.probatect.org**,#
Naturalization Indexes (partial), some loss due to 1884 fire Naturalization Records	1856 – 1906	Scanned images from original index Only on microfilm	www.probatect.org**,# (WHTC 9th floor)
Physician Certificates, vol. 3, 7, each book has index Physician Certificates, vol. 1, 2, 4, 5, 6	1919 – 1934, 1973 – 1986 1896 – 1919, 1935 – 1973	Scanned images from original books Only on microfilm Only on microfilm	www.probatect.org,# (WHTC 9th floor) "
Probate Account Records, restored**** index in each vol. (films ACR-355-363) Probate Account Records #3 to #878 index in each vol. (Films ACR 1 to 354) Account Records Probate Inventory Records, index in each vol. Probate Inventories restored indexed by HCGS**** Probate Inventories, no index index in each vol. (from films IRR-1 to 130, INV 1-62)	1843 - 1877 1852 – 1970 1961 – 1973 1809 – 1947 (incomplete) 1854 - 1881 1947 – 1963 1963 – 1973	Scanned images from original books " " " " Scanned images from original books " " " " " "	www.probatect.org**,# also at PLCH ***,# www.probatect.org**,# " www.probatect.org**,# also at PLCH *** www.probatect.org**,#
A-Z surname Index to Account and Inventory records (9,973 names)	1808 – 1883	 " " " "	www.hcgsohio.org www.probatect.org
Land Sale Appearance Docket, 1-16 Estate Sale Books	1852 – 1911 1883 – 1969	" "	www.familysearch.org (WHTC 9th floor)
Probate journal volumes, vol. 2-99 see chart on following page	1858 – 1884	Scanned images from original books	www.familysearch.org

* Some records at www.FamilySearch.org>All Record Collections>United States>Ohio Probate>Hamilton

° See also FamilySearch catalog for Hamilton County, Ohio

** Cincinnati Board of Health birth and death records, 1865-1912, and Citizenship (Naturalization) records index, 1837-1916, are online at Archives & Rare Books Library, University of Cincinnati. See www.libraries.uc.edu/libraries/arb/archives/GenealogyReference.html.

*** PLCH: Public Library of Cincinnati and Hamilton County, 8th & Vine Sts. 3rd floor, Genealogy Dept.

How-to and reference articles on use of county probate, marriage, and guardianship records can be found in the *Tracer* Articles Index, 2008-2018, at www.hcgsohio.org/cpage.php?pt=109.

**** Probates, estates, accounts, inventories: some indexed by HCGS at https://hcgsohio.org/cpage.php?pt=64.

Courthouse and County Records History

The first building used as the Hamilton County Courthouse was built about 1795 on Fifth Street between Main and Walnut. It was replaced in 1801 by a limestone building located near the southwest corner of Fifth & Main facing Fifth Street. During the War of 1812 the Courthouse was used as a military barracks and accidentally set on fire by soldiers in 1814. Virtually all of the records were destroyed during this fire. In 1818, a new Courthouse was built in the present location and it was destroyed by fire in 1849. The Courthouse was rebuilt in 1851-53 and was destroyed during a riot and fire in 1884. Many records were destroyed, and gaps were caused in others. Some records were reconstructed, restored or salvaged. Today, Hamilton County records are located in the present Courthouse, the William Howard Taft Center, the Hamilton County Administration Building, the Hamilton County General Health District on William Howard Taft Road, and the Archives and Rare Books Library at the University of Cincinnati.

In 2005, any original existing probate documents and index books before 1973 were removed from public use to be digitally scanned. In January 2010, the digital images of scanned documents and scanned microfilms were made available on the Probate Court website, www.probatect.org.

In 2011, Judge James Cissell approved a joint project between his staff and the Hamilton County Genealogical Society to create a master A-Z surname index of still existing records that survived the 1884 fire or were re-created after the fire. Indexes to probate accounts, inventories, and probate journals were completed in 2013. In 2014, the Family History Library in Salt Lake City made digital images of many probate record microfilms available on its website, FamilySearch.

Hamilton County Probate Records on FamilySearch

Administration Dockets	1852 to 1918, 57 vol.
Administration Dockets Index	1852 to 1899 (910232) 1 vol.
Administrators and Guardianship, Appointments and Bonds	Vol. 1, 1791 to 1838; Index A (image 2) to Z (image 63), page 1 is image 64, page 592 is image 366; name of deceased, date, administrator name
Administrators and Guardianship, Appointments and Bonds	Vol. 2, 1738 to 1847; Index A (image 369) to Y (image 424), page 1 is image 425, page 592 is image 721; name of deceased, date, administrator name
Determination of Heirs and Construction of Wills Docket	1959-1974 Vol. 5-6, cases 2154-3042, A-Z index
Guardians Dockets	1901 - 1907,1922 Vol. 18-19, 24
Indexes to Wills, 1 & 2	1791 - 1900; case #, name, probate date, will volume & page
Probate Journals	1858 - 1891, 42 volumes, some lost in 1884 fire
Land Sales (Appearance dockets)	1852 - 1911, vol. 1-16
Probate Minutes Index	1790 - 1852; deceased name, only surnames A to G, administrator name and dates *Brückmann, Brink*
Wills	1792 - 1918, vol. 1-140

Hamilton County Probate Journals on FamilySearch

The Family History Library (FamilySearch) is putting microfilms of records online with no aids for their use. This table identifies the pages and images for the Probate Journals. Restored Hamilton County Probate Journals, 1858 to 1890, www.FamilySearch.org>All Record Collections>United States>Ohio Probate>Hamilton

Court Microfilm	Book #	From	Book Page	FHL image #	To	Book page	FHL image #	FHL Index images	Family History Library #
JEB-224	12	8.2.1858	1	6	12.31.1858	451	236	238-261, Z-A	910207
"	17	3.12.1860	1	4	June 1860	42	25	none	910207
"	24	6.241864	1	5	9.26.1864	350	180	182-208, Z-A	910207
JEB-224	25	12.1.1864	1	6	3.27.1865	461	247	249-278, Z-A	910208
"	26	5.23.1866	1	5	1879	496	258	260-288, Z-A	910208
"	30	10.1.1866	1	5					910208
JEB-225	30 con't				1.26.1867	485	251	254-285, Z-A	910208
"	31	1.28.1867	1	5	6.18.1867	563	294	297-325, Z-A	910209
"	33	1.24.1868	1	5	4.27.1868	510	263	267-295, Z-A	910210
"	34	4.30.1868	1	302	9.2.1868	569	589	590-625, Z-A	910210
"	36	1.23.1869	1	6					910211
JEB-226	36 con't				5.19.1869	561	288	289-318, Z-A	910211
"	37	6.2.1869	1	325	10.11.1869	456	553	555-585, Z-A	910211
"	39	2.1.1870	1	5	2.8.1870	61	35	39-58, Z-A	910212
"	42	9.5.1870	1	5	12.19.1870	582	265	266-287, Z-A	910212
"	43	12.20.1870	1	6	3.27.1871	573	238	239-262, Z-A	910213
"	44	3.28.1871	1	269					910213
JEB-227	44 con't				6.21.1871	578	474	475-498, Z-A	910213
"	46	9.18.1871	1	6	12.27.1871	581	219	220-242, Z-A	910213
"	49	6.4.1872	1	5	8.12.1872	586	197	198-221, Z-A	910214
"	50	8.31.1872	1	227	10.31.1872	316	386	388-415, Z-A	910214
"	51	11.8.1872	1	5	1.25.1873	578	209	211-233, Z-A	910215
"	55	6.27.1873	1	239					910215
JEB-228	55 con't				8.13.1873	369	373	374-398, Z-A	910215
"	56	8.20.1873	1	404	10.31.1873	579	641	642-666, Z-A	910215
missing	57	12.1.1873	548	291	12.15.1873	576	305	(copied out	910216
missing	57	12.16.1873	446	240	2.19.1874	542	288	of date order)	910216
JEB-228	58	3.13.1874	1	6	5.30.1874	444	239	306-333, Z-B	910216
"	63	7.28.1875	1	5	11.6.1875	514	268	269-298, Z-A	910217
"	66	5.20.1876	1	305	8.28.1876				910217
JEB-229	66 con't					462	539	540-568, Z-A	910217
"	70	6.15.1877	1	5	9.20.1877	521	277	279-309, Z-A	910218
"	71	9.21.1877	1	315	12.28.1877	587	609	611-635, Z-A	910218
"	72	1.21.1878	1	5	4.2.1878	463	243	245-278, A-Z	910219
"	73	4.3.1878	1	284	7.2.1878	586	583	584-608, Z-A	910219
JEB-230	74	7.8.1878	1	614	10.29.1878	586	909	910-934, Z-A	910219
JEB-230	79	3.8.1879	1	5	3.28.1879	328	169	196, A-Z	910205 / 2
"	78	8.25.1879	28	20	10.9.1879	213	112	145-171, Z-A	910206
"	80	5.13.1880	214	113	5.13.1880	231	121	145-171, Z-A	910206
"	80	5.13.1880	230	128	5.19.1880	259	142	145-171, Z-A	910206
"	86	9.1.1881	1	5	11.30.1881	534	283	284-308, Z-A	910220
"	90	8.24.1882	1	6	9.23.1882	26	19	145-171, Z-A	910206
"	91	11.1.1882	1	5	1.31.1883	576	294	295-319, A-Z	910221

	92	2.1.1883	1	325	4.21.1883	583	617	618-642, A-Z	910221
JEB-231	99	8.4.1883	1	645	10.29.1883	?	660	688-712, Y-B	910223
"	95	10.17.1883	1	5	1.12.1884	588	292	300-327, A-Z	910222
"	99	1.14.1884	?	661	3.28.1884	84	687	688-712, Y-B	910223
"	97	3.29.1884	1	5	6.27.1884	577?	283	284-308, Z-A	910223
"	98	6.28.1884	1	314	9.26.1884	?	613	614-639, Z-A	910223
JEB-224	2	8.12.1884	1		1890	41	41	A-Z at front	910205/1

Hamilton County Administration Offices

138 E. Court St. (Court & Main Sts.)

Cincinnati, OH 45202-1236

M-F: 7:30 - 4:30 p.m.

OFFICE	COLLECTION	DATES	FORMAT	PLACE
County Engineer (513) 946-4250	Surveys of Properties and Roads	1793 to present	Books	Room 700
"	Hamilton County Maps County Atlas	1869 & 1884	Books & sheets	Room 700
Auditor's Office (513) 946-4000	Plat Maps	1940 - present	Book	Room 304 & online, www.hamiltoncounty auditor.org
"	Real Estate Tax Assessments			Room 304
"	Owner and address indexes			Room 304
"	Field cards indicate date building erected & first tax			Room 304
Treasurer's Office (513) 946-4800	Property Tax Records	1883 - present		Room 402
Recorder's Office (RO) (513) 946-4570 www.recordersoffice. hamilton-co.org	Deeds books A-W2, 21-400 Deed books 477 - 854 Deed books 855 to 3230 Lease books 1 - 122 Mortgages 20 - 300	1794 - 1869 1877 - 1901 1901 - 1963 1847 - 1902 1833 - 1869	Page images " " Microfilm Page images Page images	RO online** & FamilySearch* Room 205 RO & FamilySearch
"	Military Grave locations (by cemetery)	Revolutionary War to World War I	Microfiche	Room 205
"	Military Discharge Records (indexed)	Civil War - 1917 Civil War - present	Indexes Film & books	HCGS online # Room 205
"	WPA Veteran Grave Maps	Up to 1939	Cemetery map	RO online**
"	Partition Lawsuits	1800s - 1863 (Incomplete)	Microfiche	Room 205, labeled "Restored Records"
"	Township & Section Maps Plat Maps	Various 1850 to present	Book and online	Room 205
"	Field cards indicate date building erected & first tax	1937 onward by request	Cards on microfilm	Room 205

* RO collection at https://www.familysearch.org/search/collection/2141016

**RO search page, under "Document Images" at top right: https://recordersoffice.hamilton-co.org/hcro-pdi/

HCGS website: https://hcgsohio.org/cpage.php?pt=76

Hamilton County Geographical Property Transfer Books (Recorder's Office)

Series 1, books 1 to23	1794-1859	RO**		Series 5, books 1 to 66	1904-1918	RO**
Series 2, books 1 to 28	1860-1871	RO**		Series 6, books 1 to 61	1918-1927	RO**
Series 3, books 1 to 36	1872-1886	RO**		Series 7, books 1 to 85	1928-1939	RO**
Series 4, books 1 to 58	1887-1903	RO**		Series 8	1940-present	Books

Hamilton County Property Related Books

Graver, William H.:

- *Index to Selected Hamilton County, Ohio Recorder's Books, 1801-1820*
- *Hamilton County, Ohio, Guide to Recorder's Indexes and Documents, 1794-1988*

Graver, William H. and Mullen, Eileen:

- *Cincinnati, Ohio, Index to Property Owners & Streets in 1895 & 1897 Atlases: River to Liberty (Street), Freeman (Street) to Mt. Adams*
- *Hamilton County, Ohio, Index of Early Deed Books, 1804-1806 and 1814-1817*
- *Hamilton County, Ohio, Index of People, Roads, Churches, Etc. on 1835, 1847, 1848, 1869, & 1884 Maps and Atlases*

Kocher, Richard L.:

- *A Listing of Entrymen on Lands in Hamilton County, OH*

McHenry, Chris:

- *Symmes Purchase Records 1787-1800*

Smith, Alma A:

- *Ohio Lands: Hamilton County Deed Book A, 1787-1797, Territory Northwest of the River Ohio*
- *The Virginia Military Surveys of Clermont and Hamilton Counties, Ohio, 1787-1849*

Hamilton County Deed and Mortgage Books

Originals at Hamilton County Recorder's Office, 1794-1897; list compiled by W. H. Graver, 1997

This page lists the ID of each book, grouped by decade based on the date of the first recording in the book.

Microfilms of all the deed books and mortgage books can be seen at the Recorder's Office.[a] Microfilms of early deed and mortgage books can be seen at the Cincinnati History Library & Archives.

A manuscript original can be seen at the Cincinnati History Library & Archives, if the ID is in **bold type**, and/or at the Blegen Library, Archive & Rare Books Department of the University of Cincinnati, if the ID is underlined.[b]

Deed book IDs for each decade:

1790: A B1 B2 C1   1800: C2 **D1** D2 **E1 E2** F1 F2 **F3**[c] **G1**[c] H

1810: I K1[c] L M1[c] N O P Q R1 R2 S T U   1820: V1 V2 W1 W2 21-26 28-30 32 33

1830: 34 35 38 39 41-43 44 46 47 49 50 52 53 55 56 58 59 61 62 64 65 67 68 70-73

1840: **75 76 78 79 81 82 84 85 87 88 91-94 96** 97 99 100 **101** 102 104 105 107 108 **109** 111 **112 114 115** 116 **117** 119 120 **122** 123 **125** 127 **128** 129 130 133 134 136-139 142 143 145 146 148 150

1850: 151 153-155 **158 159** 162 **163** 165 166 168 **169** 171 **173** 175 **176** 178 **179** 181 182 185-187 189-192 195 197 199-202 205 206 208 209 211 212 214 216 218-220 223 224 227 228 231 232 233 235-237 239[d]-257

1860: 258-375   1870: 376-507

1880: 508-511 512-520 521-523 524-547 548 549-575 576 577-580 581-688

1890: 689-799 **780** 781-842

Mortgage books IDs for each decade:

1820: 20 27 31   1830: 36 37 40 45 48 51 54 57 60 63 66 69 74

1840: 77 80 83 86 89 **90** 95 98 103 106 110 113 118 121 124 126 131 132 135 140 141 144 147 149

1850: 152 156 157 160 161 164 167 170 172 174 177 180 183 184 188 193 194 196 198 203 204 207 210 213 215 217 221 222 225 226 229 230 234 238 239[d]-249

1860: 250-306 307 308   1870: 309-398 399 400-431

1880: 432-592   1890: 593-715 716-765

[a] If a page is illegible on the microfilm, ask in the Photo Room to see an aperture card or the manuscript book if it's available.

[b] A few days' notice is necessary for UC to get these books from their out-of-town remote storage.

[c] Some indexes refer to this book by its letter alone (that is: F, G, K or M).

[d] Note that beginning with number 239 there is a book for every number in both deeds and mortgages. Numbers 20-238 were assigned as needed to either a deed or a mortgage book. The deed books with IDs A to W2 are all-document books.

Hamilton County Clerk of Courts

1000 Main St. (at Court St.)

Cincinnati, OH 45202-1206

M-F: 8-4 p.m.

OFFICE	COLLECTION	DATES	FORMAT	PLACE
Common Pleas Clerk of Courts (513) 946-5606	Naturalization Records	1850-1893	Microfilm or Microfiche	Paper Room 315
"	Declaration of Intent	1842-1926	"	"
"	Court Dockets	1884-present	"	"
"	Certified Judgments	1884-present	"	"
"	Pending Suits	1884-present	"	"
"	Judgments	1884-present	"	"
"	Law Suits & Divorces	1884-1994	"	"
"	Criminal & Civil Records	1884-present	"	"

Naturalizations and some other county records have been moved to the Archives & Rare Books Library located in the Carl Blegen Library at the University of Cincinnati. See partial list on pages 8-9.

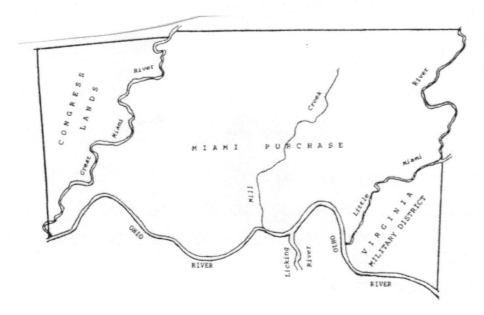

Hamilton County is in three of Ohio's original subdivisions: Congress Lands (1798-1801), Miami Purchase (1794), Virginia Military District (1784).

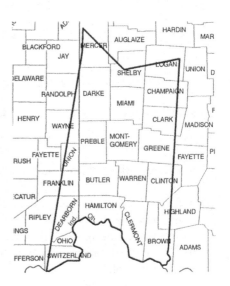

Hamilton County, 1798

Tracer Articles about Court and Land Records

Court records

"Historic Hamilton County Courts and Their Records," June 2014

"Early Hamilton County Common Pleas Court Records and How to Find a Particular Case," September 2014

"Superior Court of Cincinnati: Early Records Uncovered and Demystified," December 2014

"Destruction of Hamilton County Courthouse Records," December 2016

"Law Publications with Hamilton County Cases," March 2019

Divorce

"Ohio and Hamilton County Divorce Records," March 2014

"Divorce Records of the Insolvency Court, 1909-1914," June 2014; "Update," December 2015

Land records

"Hamilton County Recorder's Office Early Indexes and Records," September 2012

"Using Hamilton County Geographical Deed and Mortgage Indexes on FamilySearch," Part 1, September 2014; Part 2, December 2014

"Speculators, Surveys and Deeds," March 2017

"Hamilton County Deeds, 1788-1857," March 2017

"Hamilton County Recorder: Ancestral Leases and Liens Now Online," December 2017

Probate records

"Hamilton County Probate Records: Online at Last!", February 2010

"Hamilton County Probate Accounts – Why Look at Them?", August 2011

"Hamilton County Probate Journals – Why Look at Them?", December 2012

"Three Online Collections of Hamilton County Probate Records," March 2014

"*More* Hamilton County Probate Court Records," March 2015

Chapter 5: Other Records

Census Records

This list consolidates the types of census records available for Hamilton County, surviving years, and record locations. Ancestry can be used free of charge at any branch of the Public Library of Cincinnati and Hamilton County (PLCH) and LDS Family History Centers. PLCH card-holders can use HeritageQuest on any computer.

Population census, 1820-1940

- Ancestry, U.S. Census Schedules: indexed images
- PLCH: microfilm and index books
- FamilySearch: indexed images
- HeritageQuest: indexed images

Non-population census

Agricultural schedules, 1850, 1860, 1870

These schedules enumerate farm owners, agents, and managers, with details about acreage, crops, livestock, and machinery. Each entry is one line on two pages.

- Ancestry, U.S., Selected Federal Census Non-Population Schedules, 1850-1880: indexed images
- PLCH: microfilm

Defective, dependent, and delinquent schedules, 1880

This schedule has different forms to enumerate details about these individuals: "insane, idiots, deafmutes, blind, paupers and indigent persons, homeless children, prisoners."

- Ancestry, U.S. Federal Census - 1880 Schedules of Defective, Dependent, and Delinquent Classes: indexed images
- PLCH: microfilm

Industry schedules, 1850, 1870, 1880

These schedules enumerate manufacturers grossing over $500 a year including those who operated on a small scale, like shoemakers and tanners. Information includes capital invested, raw material, power, employees, and annual products.

- Ancestry, U.S., Selected Federal Census Non-Population Schedules, 1850-1880: indexed images
- PLCH: microfilm

Mortality schedules, 1850, 1860

These schedules enumerate people who died in the periods of May 31, 1849 to June 1, 1850 and May 31, 1859 to June 1, 1860. Information includes name, age, color, married or widowed, state or country of birth, month of death, occupation, cause of death, and number of days ill. Some items may be omitted.

- Ancestry, U.S. Federal Census Mortality Schedules, 1850-1885: indexed images
- PLCH: microfilm

"Deaf Family Marriages and Hearing Relatives," 1888-1895

Four-page questionnaires sent to deaf couples and family members of deaf individuals asked for information on three generations of the family—the couple's parents and siblings, the married couple, and their children. This is not an official census but the information is valuable.

- Ancestry, U.S. Special Census on Deaf Family Marriages and Hearing Relatives, 1888-1895: indexed images

Veterans' schedules, 1890

These schedules enumerate Union Army veterans and their widows, with details including rank, military unit, enlistment and discharge dates, disabilities, residence, etc.

- Ancestry, 1890 Veterans Schedules: indexed images
- PLCH: microfilm
- HCGS book: *Index to Hamilton County, Ohio, Special Census: 1890 Union Veterans & Widows of the Civil War*, Margie and Michael Mohr

State census

Ohio does not have any state census records. Quadrennial enumerations from 1804 to 1907 recorded men 21 and older every four years to determine legislative districts, but none survive for Hamilton County.

1850 mortality census, Hamilton County; note cholera deaths

City and County Directories

Directories are available in book form or microfilm at the Public Library of Cincinnati and Hamilton County and at the Cincinnati History Library and Archives. Many directories are also digitized in the PLCH Digital Library.

Unexpected extras

1819	A 90-page history section is included in the first Cincinnati directory.
1825	Place of nativity is given for each person. The reprinted booklet version adds an index to "text and to names hidden within the regular entries of the directory."
1829	A table of deaths by age and causes is on page 202.
1834, 1840 1842, 1844	Each has a separate alphabetical listing for colored persons.

1834, 1840, 1860, 1861, 1866, 1867, 1869, 1872, 1874

Separate alphabetical listings for Covington, KY, and Newport, KY.

1840	State or country of birth is given for each person. There is also a separate alphabetical listing for Fulton, a short-lived township running from the then boundary of Cincinnati eastward along the Ohio River.
1842	Separate alphabetical listing for each political ward instead of a single list for the whole city.
1853	In his introduction to this issue, C. S. Williams discusses "the numbering of the houses" in the city. He also includes *Cincinnati As It Is* to give a very short sketch of the Past."
1857	Williams' preface explains the effects of some recent street name changes.
1863	This year's preface reveals information about people in the midst of the Civil War.
1872, 1874	Each has a separate alphabetical listing for Bellevue, KY, and Dayton, KY.
1889	New names of streets begin on page lxxii. Six pages of the old street names and the changes begin on page lxvii.
1896	First directory with modern house numbers, i.e., 400 Broadway is at the intersection of 4th Street.
1905	First directory to designate military service of city residents as USA, US Army; USN, US Navy; or US Marine after the individual's name. By WWI the designations USA, USN, and USM are standard. Some directories note if the service member was in the reserves.
1911-1913	Separate street directory for annexed villages.
1923	First directory listing every house number with name of the head of household.

Cincinnati city directories, 1819 to present

1819, 1825, 1829, 1831, 1834, 1836/37, 1840, 1842, 1843, 1844, 1846, 1849/50, 1850/51, 1851/52, 1853, 1855 to 1925, 1926/27 to 1933/34, 1935, 1936/37, 1938 to present.

Beginning in 1938, the name of the wife is shown in parentheses.

The available Cincinnati city directories from 1819 to 1949 are downloadable and searchable in the PLCH Digital Library at https://digital.cincinnatilibrary.org/digital/collection/p16998coll5. The Digital Library also has most of the Norwood and Hamilton County directories.

Norwood, Ohio, city directories, 1896-1954

1896, 1902, 1909/10, 1911/12, 1913/14, 1915/16, 1917/18, 1919/20, 1922/23, 1924/25, 1926/27, 1928/29, 1930/31, 1932/33, 1934/35, 1937/38, 1939, 1942, 1944, 1954.

Hamilton County, Ohio, directories

1887-1915

These books have separate alphabetical lists for each town and village and one for the rest of the county outside of Cincinnati. 1887, 1889, 1891, 1893, 1897, 1899, 1901, 1905, 1907/8, 1909/10, 1911/12, 1915.

1939-1964

These books have one alphabetical list for the entire county outside of Cincinnati. A town, village, or township is noted for each person and business. 1939, 1940, 1942, 1944, 1946, 1957-1964.

Other directories

Many are available in the Digital Library at https://digital.cincinnatilibrary.org/digital/collection/p16998coll13.

- Cincinnati Business Directories: 1844, 1846, 1848/1849, 1851/1852, 1857/1858, 1866, 1867, 1893, 1895, 1897/1898, 1901-1913, 1915-1918.
- Illustrated Business Directories and Picturesque Cincinnati: 1882-1900, 1902.
- Specialized directories for musicians; builders; river workers; physicians, dentists, and druggists.
- Cincinnati Suburban Directories: 1965 to present.

Resources

City and County Directories web page on the HCGS website, https://hcgsohio.org/cpage.php?pt=65

"Cincinnati and Hamilton County Directories," *The Tracer,* September 2006

German Records and Resources

The German Interest Group's page on the HCGS website, https://hcgsohio.org/cpage.php?pt=190, has more information about these topics including links to indexes and records. See the HCGS blog, 16 October 2018, for a post with many links to German websites (https://hcgsohio.blogspot.com/search?q=german+genealogy).

Cemeteries

The HCGS Cemeteries page, https://hcgsohio.org/cpage.php?pt=63, has information about Hamilton County cemeteries. These large cemeteries are predominantly German:

- Baltimore Pike Cemetery (Protestant)
- Calvary Cemetery (Catholic)
- Old St. Joseph, St. Mary, St. John Cemeteries (Catholic)
- Vine Street Hill Cemetery (Protestant)
- Walnut Hills Cemetery (Protestant)
- Walnut Hills United Jewish Cemetery

"German Genealogy Books Available for Use"

Accessed from the HCGS web page, this 58-page guide lists books and articles to assist researchers in discovering their German ancestors, including many for Cincinnati and Hamilton County. The resources are listed in categories such as German research guides, German immigration records, German periodicals, and German articles in *The Tracer*, among many others.

Indexes

Index of Lesser Known German Resources, by Marilyn Wood Armstrong, Beverly Igel Breitenstein, and Jeffrey G. Herbert, includes many birthplaces found in these records:

- Descriptive book of the 9th Regiment Ohio Volunteer Infantry
- Cincinnati Central Turner Society membership lists
- Every-name index to three Cincinnati histories in German: *Cincinnati und sein Deutschthum, Cincinnati in Word und Bild, Cincinnati Sonst und Jetzt*

Newspapers

HCGS has published indexes to nearly 120,000 death notices in five German newspapers before 1920 and posted them on its website (complete information for members, abbreviated for non-members). See https://hcgsohio.org/cpage.php?pt=62.

- *Christliche Apologete,* 1839-1899 (German Methodist)
- *Freie Presse,* 1874-1920
- *Volksblatt,* 1846-1918
- *Volksfreund,* 1850-1908
- *Zeitung,* 1887-1901

Oldenburg Catholic records

Many Cincinnati Germans came from the Oldenburg area of the Diocese of Münster, Germany. Images of its Catholic parish records are available for free browsing at Matricula, http://data.matricula-online.eu/en. For more information, see the HCGS blog, 19 February 2019, https://hcgsohio.blogspot.com/search?q=matricula.

Orphanages

- The German General Protestant Orphan Home was founded in 1849.
- The St. Aloysius Orphan Asylum, a German Catholic orphanage, was founded in 1837. Until 1917 only children who spoke German were admitted.

Societies

The surviving records of German societies such as the Deutsche Pionier Verein, the largest German society in Cincinnati, contain valuable information such as birthplace, immigration, and other details. For more details about German societies, see "The Records of German Societies in Hamilton County," *The Tracer* (August 2016).

Videos for HCGS members

Log in to the HCGS website to view these videos.

- "Researching Your German Ancestors Using German Newspapers," parts 1 and 2, Jeff Herbert (2014)
- "What's New in German Research," Jeff Herbert (2018)

Societies and collections with German resources

- Cincinnati Family History Center,
  https://www.familysearch.org/wiki/en/Cincinnati_Ohio_Family_History_Center
- German-American Citizens League's German Heritage Museum, http://www.gacl.org/page3.html
- German-Americana Collection, http://libraries.uc.edu/arb/collections/german-americana.html
- International German Genealogy Partnership, https://iggpartner.org/index.php
- Public Library of Cincinnati and Hamilton County, https://www.cincinnatilibrary.org

Seit Gründung des Vereins sind sechs Mitglieder gestorben, nämlich:

Jacob Hanhaufer aus Langenkantel in Baiern, geboren den 13. März 1809, ausgewandert von Havre, den 29. September 1835 gelandet in New-York, nach Cincinnati gekommen den 3. Dez. 1835, gestorben am 6. August 1868.

Valentin Bruck aus Mendel in Kurheffen, geboren den 17. Febr. 1815, ausgewandert von Havre den 20. April 1837, gelandet in New York am 10. Juni 1837, in Cincinnati angekommen im Mai 1851, gestorben am 8 October 1868.

Johann G. Hagen, aus Meringen in Baden, geboren den 26. 1803, ausgewandert von Havre den 17. Februar 1837, gelandet in New-Orleans den 9. Juni 1837, in Cincinnati angekommen den 18. Juli 1837, gest. den 29. Nov. 1868

Biographical information in Der Deutsche Pionier

Naturalization Records

Searching for records in "Ohio, County Naturalization Records, 1800-1977"

FamilySearch volunteers have indexed nearly 40,000 naturalization records that mention Hamilton County, so first try a search at https://www.familysearch.org/search/collection/1987615, "Ohio, County Naturalization Records." However, it's not known if the collection is completely indexed. Don't stop there if a name isn't found.

Use the process below to search the images of Hamilton County naturalization records that have not yet been indexed in "Ohio County Naturalizations." All four steps are needed only if a record isn't found in prior steps.

Step 1

Search the Hamilton County Citizenship Records index on the Archives and Rare Books website, https://libraries.uc.edu/arb/collections/local-government/naturalization.html, or Lois Hughes, *Hamilton County, Ohio Citizenship Record Abstracts, 1837-1916* (Bowie, MD: Heritage Books, 1991). **This index is incomplete**.

If a name is found, use the volume and page number to locate the record on FamilySearch. A list of the exact dates, volume numbers, and microfilm numbers for each set of naturalization images clarifies the generic record titles and overlapping date ranges on FamilySearch (see pages 55-56).

- Volumes 1-18: Declarations of intention, 1848-1862, 1871-73
- Volumes 19, 21: Declarations of intention, 1885-1895 (no Volume 20 entries in the index)
- Volumes 22-27: Declarations of intention, 1848, 1849, 1852, 1856, 1860
- Volume 28: Special naturalizations, 1887-1926

If no volume number is given, check the alphabetical record series on FamilySearch (step 3).

Step 2

Search https://www.probatect.org/court-records/archive-categories/naturalizations, the 1856-1906 Naturalization Indexes on the Probate Court website. For names found with J in the first index volume, or any names in the second index volume, use the volume and page number to locate the Probate Journal record in "Ohio Probate Records" on FamilySearch (https://www.familysearch.org/search > Collection Title: Ohio Probate Records > Browse > Hamilton). An essential finding aid for records coded as J is a list showing Probate Journal volumes, dates, page numbers, and image numbers (see pages 40-41).

The remaining naturalization records covered by the indexes on the Probate Court website (preserved and restored declarations and naturalizations of aliens, minors, and soldiers) are digitized on FamilySearch in "Ohio, Hamilton County Records" (see pages 57-58).

Step 3

Search three sets of alphabetically filed naturalization records on FamilySearch by browsing rather than using the search box, at https://www.familysearch.org/search/catalog/85624?availability=Family%20History%20Library.

- Declarations of Intention, 1850-1902
- Post-naturalization Records, 1850-1902
- Declarations of Intention, 1880-1890, A-M, N-Z

Step 4

Search four sets of naturalization records with internal indexes on FamilySearch at https://www.familysearch.org/search/catalog/732036?availability=Family%20History%20Library, by browsing rather than using the search box. These are the same records indexed in the Hamilton County Citizenship Records index on the Archives and Rare Books site and Lois Hughes, *Hamilton County, Ohio Citizenship Record Abstracts, 1837-1916.*

- Declarations of Intention, 1848-1873
- Declarations of Intention, 1848, 1849, 1852, 1856, 1860
- Declarations of Intention, 1885-1895
- Special Naturalizations, 1887-1926

Searching for records in "Ohio, Southern District Naturalization Index, 1852-1991"

Search the FamilySearch card index for naturalizations in the U.S. District Court, Southern District of Ohio, Western Division, in Cincinnati. Many residents of large cities like Cincinnati chose to file in federal rather than local courts. None of the record titles on FamilySearch refer to the name of the court where the records were filed. Try the search box at https://www.familysearch.org/search/collection/2110749?collectionNameFilter=true and browse the images if records aren't found. The Cincinnati indexes are listed below:

- 1852-1892
- 1906-1986, Aakhus – Bui
- 1906-1986, Bujak – Ghizas
- 1906-1986, Ghouri – Kron
- 1906-1986, Kronberger – O'Sullivan
- 1906-1986, Osuszt – Simons
- 1906-1986, Simonsen – Zysset

For more information about searching images of naturalization records, see "Hamilton County Online Naturalization Records and Indexes" in the June and September 2013 issues of *The Tracer*.

Other naturalization records are in "Hamilton County, Ohio, Records" on FamilySearch and on the Probate Court website. See pages 57-58.

Offline naturalization records

The records indexed by the U.S. District Court cards on FamilySearch as well as U.S. Circuit Court records (1852-1905) are held by the National Archives and Records Administration facility in Chicago. See "Hamilton County Naturalization Records Filed in Federal Courts, 1852-1990, and All Courts, 1906-1956" in the August 2009 issue of *The Tracer* for information about the types of records at NARA and the ordering process.

The office of the U. S. District Court in downtown Cincinnati has indexes and some original naturalization records after 1956. The phone number is 513-564-7500.

U.S. Citizenship and Immigration Services (https://www.uscis.gov/genealogy) will search its post-1906 record indexes (containing about 48 million entries) for all citations related to a specific immigrant. The cost of an index search for one individual is $20. With the citation, copies of records can be obtained for $25.

Naturalization Records on FamilySearch and LDS Microfilm
with Volume Numbers, FamilySearch Titles, and Archives and Rare Books (UC) Index References

FamilySearch Title and Order	Court Dates	Vol.	LDS Film #	Comments
Declarations of intention 1848	27 Jul – 9 Oct 1848	1	1415172	UC: Vol. 22
Declarations of intention 1848-1849	2 Oct 1848 – 31 Jan 1849	1	1415117	UC: Vol. 1
Declarations of intention 1849-1850	1 Feb 1849 – 28 Jun 1850	3	1415172	UC: Vol. 23
Declarations of intention 1850-1851	28 Jan 1850 – 30 Jan 1851; 19 Apr 1850 – 30 Jul 1851	2 3	1415117	Two volumes in one set; UC: Vol. 2 & 3
Declarations of intention 1850-1902 A-Z	1850-1902	-	1402982	
Declarations of intention 1850-1902 Anders - Cohen	1850-1902	-	14202975	
Declarations of intention 1850-1902 Coghlan – Grosser	1850-1902	-	14202976	
Declarations of intention 1850-1902 Grosser – Jurgen	1850-1902	-	14202977	
Declarations of intention 1850-1902 Kaiser – McPartlin	1850-1902	-	1402978	
Declarations of intention 1850-1902 McPartlin – Rieding	1850-1902	-	1402979	
Declarations of intention 1850-1902 Riedinger – Sterzer	1850-1902	-	1402980	
Declarations of intention 1850-1902 Sterzer - Zwosta	1850-1902	-	1402981	
Declarations of intention 1851	18 Jul – 23 Dec 1851	4	1415118	UC: Vol. 4
Declarations of intention 1851-1852	24 Dec 1851 – 10 May 1852	7	1415172	UC: Vol. 24
Declarations of intention 1852	10 May 1852 – 15 Sep 1852	8	1415173	UC: Vol. 25
Declarations of intention 1852-1853	16 Oct 1852 – 10 Jan 1853	5	1415118	UC: Vol. 5
Declarations of intention 1852-1854	7 Oct – 10 Oct 1854; 1 Nov – 17 Nov 1852	8	1415120	Pages 1-240 Pages 241-426 UC: Vol. 8
Declarations of intention 1853	10 Jan – 4 Apr 1853	6	1415118	UC: Vol. 6
Declarations of intention 1853-1854	4 Apr – 23 May 1853; 17 Apr – 25 May 1854	7	1415118	UC: Vol. 7
Declarations of intention 1854	5 Jun – 7 Oct 1854; 5 Jun 1854 – 7 Oct 1854; 17 Apr 1854 – 3 Jun 1854	9 10 11	1415119	Three volumes in one set UC: Vol. 9, 10, 11
Declarations of intention 1854-1855	7 Oct 1854 – 11 Sep 1855	12	1415120	UC: Vol. 12
Declarations of intention 1855-1856	11 Sep 1855 – 2 Feb 1856	13	1415121	UC: Vol. 13
Declarations of intention 1856	2 Feb 1856 – 28 May 1856	16	1415173	UC: Vol. 26
Declarations of intention 1856-1857	29 Sep 1856 – 7 Feb 1857	14	1415121	UC: Vol. 14
Declarations of intention 1857	9 Feb – 9 Nov 1857	15	1415121	UC: Vol. 15
Declarations of intention 1857-1858	9 Nov 1857 – 2 Aug 1858	16	1415122	UC: Vol. 16

FamilySearch Title and Order	Court Dates	Vol.	LDS Film #	Comments
Declarations of intention 1858-1859	29 Oct 1858 – 31 Dec 1859	17	1415122	UC: Vol. 17
Declarations of intention 1860	25 Jun – 2 Nov 1860	-	1415173	UC: Vol. 27
Declarations of intention 1860-1873	2 Nov 1860 – 1 Sep 1862; 1 Nov 1871 – 24 Feb 1873	18	1415122	UC: Vol. 18
Declarations of intention 1880-1890 A-M	1880-1890	-	1415174	
Declarations of intention 1880-1890 N-Z	1880-1890	-	1415175	
Declarations of intention 1885-1893	16 Feb 1885 – 11 Oct 1893	19	1415123	UC: Vol. 19
Declarations of intention 1893-1895	12 Oct 1893 – 23 Oct 1895	20	1415123	No Vol. 20 in UC; must be UC Vol. 21
Naturalization index 1864-1908	1856-1906; 1848-1884	1	1415171	www.probatect.org
Naturalization index 1880-1890	1880-1899	-	1415124	
Naturalization index 1880-1899	1880-1899	-	1763584	Duplicate
Post naturalization records 1850-1902 Albert – Bosche	1850-1902	-	1402983	LDS "Re-application records 1850-1902"
Post naturalization records 1850-1902 Bosse – Claver	1850-1902	-	1402984	LDS "Re-application records 1850-1902"
Post naturalization records 1850-1902 Cleary – Dunhoft	1850-1902	-	1402985	LDS "Re-application records 1850-1902"
Post naturalization records 1850-1902 Dunn – Flocken	1850-1902	-	1402986	LDS "Re-application records 1850-1902"
Post naturalization records 1850-1902 Flory – Haumesser	1850-1902	-	1402987	LDS "Re-application records 1850-1902"
Post naturalization records 1850-1902 Hausman – Joseph	1850-1902	-	1402988	LDS "Re-application records 1850-1902"
Post naturalization records 1850-1902 Joseph – Kunz	1850-1902	-	1402989	LDS "Re-application records 1850-1902"
Post naturalization records 1850-1902 Kunz – Mead	1850-1902	-	1402990	LDS "Re-application records 1850-1902"
Post naturalization records 1850-1902 Meier – O'Ken	1850-1902	-	1402991	LDS "Re-application records 1850-1902"
Post naturalization records 1850-1902 Oker – Runge	1850-1902	-	1402992	LDS "Re-application records 1850-1902"
Post naturalization records 1850-1902 Rurve – Smith	1850-1902	-	1402993	LDS "Re-application records 1850-1902"
Post naturalization records 1850-1902 Sneath – Walsh	1850-1902	-	1402994	LDS "Re-application records 1850-1902"
Post naturalization records 1850-1902 Walsh – Zucker	1850-1902	-	1402995	LDS "Re-application records 1850-1902"
Post naturalization records 1887-1926	1887-1926	-	1415125	UC: Vol. 28; "Restoration of Naturalization Papers, 1887-1926"
Special naturalizations	1887-1926	-	1763579	Duplicate

Naturalizations on Probate Court's Website
and in "Ohio, Hamilton County Records" on FamilySearch

Probate Court naturalization records (https://www.probatect.org/court-records/archive-categories/naturalizations) have been enhanced and have better quality than the FamilySearch images of the same records, for the most part. With an index reference, go directly to the volume and page number of the record.

For naturalizations in "Ohio, Hamilton County Records, 1791-1994" on FamilySearch (https://www.familysearch.org/search/collection/2141016), click Browse and choose Naturalization Records, then select a title and start browsing the images.

Partial index to these records

Images of two index books are available on the same Probate Court website. Naturalization Index Volume 1 is in true alphabetical order. Along with volume and page number, this typed index has code letters: R for a Restored record, J for a Journal [Probate] record, CP for a Common Pleas record, M for a minor, and S for a soldier.

Naturalization Index Volume 2 is in alphabetical order by the first letter of the surname, then chronological by date of naturalization, with volume and page numbers. The names appear to be the same names as those in Volume 1 that have a J for [Probate] Journal placed before the volume number.

Years	Probate Court title	FamilySearch title	Volume	Contents
1856-1859 1864-1866	Preserved declarations of aliens	Declarations of intention	1, 4	Alien's name, native country, age, ruler of country, emigration port and date, immigration port and date, signature, date of oath of allegiance.
1875	Preserved declarations of aliens	Declarations of intention	14	Same as above
1877-1880	Preserved declarations of aliens	Declarations of intention	17-18	Same as above
1884-1906	Preserved declarations of aliens	Declarations of intention	22-45	Same as above
1884-1900	Restored declarations of aliens	Declarations of intention	1-3	Province and country, age, emigration port and date, arrival port and date, length of residence in Hamilton County, original date of declaration, witness testimony.
1880-1906	Record books	Petitions for naturalization	3-48	Witness testimony, date and court where applicant declared his intention to become a citizen, judge's order to admit the applicant as a citizen.
1884-1894	Record A-books [military]	Petitions for naturalization	A-1	Details about immigration and military service, witness testimony, applicant's signature, enlistment and discharge dates, company and regiment, and reason for discharge. Many applicants served in the Civil War.

Years	Probate Court title	FamilySearch title	Volume	Contents
1883-1892	Record A-books	Petitions for naturalization	A-6 to A-24	Witness testimony, details about the date and court where the applicant declared his intention to become a citizen, and the judge's order to admit the applicant as a citizen.
1894-1903	Soldiers	Special naturalizations (military)	1 (FHL vol. A-25)	Names, countries of origin, ages, military units, enlistment and discharge dates of aliens honorably discharged from the U.S. Army.
1903-1906	Soldiers	Special naturalizations (military)	2-3	Same as above
1903-1904	Minors [certificates]	Special naturalizations (minors)	25	Names of parents or guardians, ages and countries of origin of applicants, their oaths of allegiance, and the testimonies of witnesses.
1905-1906	Minors applications	Special naturalizations (minors)	25-27	These applicants immigrated when they were under age 18 and applied for citizenship when they were over 21. Names of parents or guardians, countries of origin, ages and dates of arrival of applicants.
1884-1942	Restored books (vols. 2-13)	Special naturalizations (restored)	2-13 (FHL vols. 1-13)	Requests for restoration of certificates destroyed in the courthouse fire, including alien's name, native country, age, ruler of country, emigration port and date, arrival port and date, date of declaration of intention, date of naturalization.

Newspapers

Microfilm in PLCH Magazines and Newspapers Department

Catholic Telegraph	Oct. 22, 1831 – Nov. 8, 1996
Centinel of the Northwestern Territory*	Nov. 9, 1793 – May 14, 1796
Cincinnati Abend-Post	Oct. 22, 1878 – Oct. 24, 1880
Cincinnati Advertiser	Jun., 1818 – Jun., 1840
(Shelved with Cincinnati Enquirer)	
Cincinnati American	Oct., 1913 – Feb. 26, 1914
Cincinnati Anzeiger	Nov. 4, 1880 – Oct. 20, 1901
Cincinnati Chronicle	Apr. 22, 1837 – Sep. 24, 1842
Cincinnati Chronicle and Literary Gazette*	Jan., 1830 – Sep., 1837
Cincinnati Commercial*	Oct., 1866 – Dec., 1882
Cincinnati Commercial Gazette*	Jan., 1883 – Jun., 1896
Cincinnati Commercial Tribune	Jul., 1896 – Dec. 3, 1930
Cincinnati Daily Chronicle	Dec., 1869 – Jun., 1871
Cincinnati Daily Columbian	Jun. 19, 1854 – Sep. 10, 1856
Cincinnati Daily Commercial*	Jan., 1858 – Sep., 1866
Cincinnati Daily Gazette* (a.k.a. Cincinnati Gazette)	Jun. 26, 1827 – Dec., 1881
Cincinnati Daily Nonpareil*	Nov., 1851 – May, 1852
Cincinnati Daily Star	Jan. 16, 1860 – Oct. 15, 1875
Cincinnati Enquirer*	Jun., 1818 – present
(Called Cincinnati Advertiser Jun., 1818 – Jun., 1840)	
Cincinnati Freie Presse*	Aug., 1874 – Jun. 9, 1964
Cincinnati Herald	Mar. 17, 1961 – Dec., 1994
Cincinnati Morning Chronicle	Mar 8, 1848 – May, 1848
(March issues filmed with Daily Cincinnati Chronicle)	
Cincinnati Morning Herald	Oct. 5, 1843 – Jul., 1844; Jan., 1845 – Nov. 27, 1845
Cincinnati Post	Jul., 1882 - present
(Includes issues entitled "Post and Times-Star")	
Cincinnati Tageblatt	Jul. 22, 1895 – Oct. 17, 1896
Cincinnati Tägliche Morgen-Post	Dec. 3, 1877 – Oct. 12, 1878
Cincinnati Times-Star	Apr. 25, 1840 – Jul., 1958
(Earlier issues entitled "Spirit of the Times," "Daily Times," and "Times and Chronicle")	
Cincinnati Tribune	Jan. 4, 1893 – Jun., 1896
Cincinnati Volksblatt*	Jan. 16, 1846 – Mar. 30, 1918
Cincinnati Volksfreund*	Jan., 1854 – Jun. 11, 1908
Cincinnati Weekly Chronicle	1869
Cincinnati Weekly Enquirer	Jul. 8, 1868 – Feb. 9, 1921
Cincinnati Weekly Gazette	Jan., 1878 – 1881
Cincinnati Weekly News	Jan., 1883 – Jun. 11, 1884
Cincinnati Weekly Star	Mar. 14, 1872 – Jun. 23, 1880
Cincinnati Weekly Times	Aug. 16, 1886 – Dec., 1889
Cincinnatier Zeitung*	Jul., 1887 – Oct. 20, 1901
Commoner	Jan. 23, 1901 – Apr., 1923
Daily Atlas (Cincinnati)	Jul. 3, 1848 – Jun., 1849
Daily Chronicle & Atlas (Cincinnati)	1850
Daily Cincinnati Atlas	Jan. 3, 1854 – Jun. 30, 1854

* Death and other notices indexed by Hamilton County Genealogical Society

Daily Cincinnati Chronicle	Jul., 1847 – Feb. 26, 1848
Daily Cincinnati Morning Chronicle	Feb. 28, 1848 – Mar. 7, 1848
(Filed with Daily Cincinnati Chronicle)	
Daily Cincinnati Republican*	Sep. 7, 1840 – Aug., 1842
Daily Dispatch (Cincinnati)*	Jun. 5, 1849 – Apr., 1850
Daily Times (See Cincinnati Times-Star)*	
Dollar Weekly Times (Cincinnati)	Aug. 26, 1852 – Oct. 27, 1864
Evening Telegram (Cincinnati)	Oct. 19, 1885 – Feb. 7, 1889
Frank Leslie's Illustrated Newspaper	1865, 1873 – 1874
Freeman's Journal*	Mar 4, 1796 – Feb. 23, 1813
Harrison News	1871 – 1927
Mercantile Daily Advertiser (Cincinnati)	Sep. 5, 1826 – Nov., 1826
National Crisis and Cincinnati Emporium	Jan., 1827 – Oct. 13, 1828
National Republican and Cincinnati Daily Mercantile Advertiser*	Mar. 25, 1831 – Jul. 9, 1833
Norwood Enterprise	Jan. 2, 1930 – Dec. 25, 1967
(Not complete – some days/months/years missing)	
Norwood News	Jan., 1930 – Dec., 1962
(Not complete – some days/months/years missing)	
Ohio Phoenix	Jan. 3, 1835 – Dec. 31, 1836
Protestantisches Zeitblätter	1853-1865
Spirit of the Times (See Cincinnati Times-Star)	
Spirit of the West (Cincinnati)*	Jul. 26, 1814 – Apr. 29, 1815
Sun (Cincinnati)	Jun. 8, 1884 – Feb. 1, 1887; Apr. 28, 1944 –Dec. 23, 1955
Times and Chronicle (See Cincinnati Times-Star)	
Union (Cincinnati)	Oct. 5, 1915 – Sep. 22, 1923
West and South (Cincinnati)	Sep. 26, 1865 – Sep. 12, 1868
Western Fountain (Cincinnati)	Mar. 21, 1850 – Sep. 18, 1851
Western Spy (Cincinnati)*	May 28, 1799 – Dec. 28, 1822
Westliche Blätter (Cincinnati; see Volksblatt)*	Nov. 5, 1865 – Mar. 31, 1918

Death and other notices indexed by Hamilton County Genealogical Society

Digitized in PLCH Digital Library

Digitized newspapers can be accessed through the PLCH home page, https://www.cincinnatilibrary.org, Research and Homework > Research Databases > Genealogy. A library card is required for access to these materials.

Newsbank: Cincinnati Post	1882 - 1990
Proquest Historical Newspapers: The Cincinnati Enquirer	1841 - 2009

More recent newspapers can be accessed through Research Databases > Magazine & Newspaper Articles.

News Bank: Cincinnati Post	1990-2007
ProQuest Digitized Newspapers: The Cincinnati Enquirer Recent	2010 – recent (3-month embargo)

This newspaper can be accessed through the Digital Library, https://digital.cincinnatilibrary.org. No library card is required.

Catholic Telegraph	1831 – 1930

Ohio History Connection

Digitized newspapers can be accessed at https://ohiomemory.ohiohistory.org/newspapers. Sort by county.

Cincinnati Daily Press	1880 – 1882
Cincinnati Daily Star	1875 – 1880
Daily Press	1859 – 1859
Labor Advocate	1915 – 1917
Ohio Organ of the Temperance Reform	1853 – 1854
Organ of the Temperance Reform	1852 – 1863
Penny Press	1859 – 1860
Star	1875 – 1875
Tägliches Cincinnatier Volksblatt	1910 – 1918
Westliche Blätter	1865 – 1885

Tracer articles

- "Hamilton County Genealogy in Nineteenth-Century Religious Newspapers," March 2013
- "Researching Early Ancestors in Hamilton County Newspapers," June 2015
- "Hamilton County Newspaper Indexes and Resources," June 2015
- "*Der Christliche Apologete*: A National German Methodist Newspaper," August 2016

HCGS newspaper indexes: published and online

HCGS member Jeffrey G. Herbert has compiled indexes for the following newspapers. Some are on the HCGS website. Non-members get abbreviated access while members get full access. For more information, see the Death Notices and Obituaries web page, https://hcgsohio.org/cpage.php?pt=62, and the Court Records web page, https://hcgsohio.org/cpage.php?pt=182.

- 23 Early Cincinnati Newspapers 1793-1853 (deaths, marriages, miscellaneous)
- Cincinnati Commercial 1858-1899 (death notices)
- Cincinnati Daily Gazette 1827-1881 (death notices and marriage notices)
- Cincinnati Daily Times 1840-1879 (death notices)
- Cincinnati Enquirer 1818-1869 (death and marriage notices)
- Cincinnati Enquirer 1841-1869; 1870-1879 (court cases)
- Cincinnati Freie Presse 1874-1920 (death and other notices)
- Cincinnati Volksblatt 1846-1918 (death notices and marriage notices)
- Cincinnati Volksfreund 1850-1908 (death notices and marriage notices)
- Cincinnatier Zeitung 1887-1901 (death lists)
- Der Christliche Apologete, 1839-1899 (death notices)
- Liberty Hall and Cincinnati Gazette 1804-1857 (death, marriage and miscellaneous notices)

Orphan Asylum Records

Over one hundred thousand children spent part of their childhood in nineteen Hamilton County orphan asylums in the nineteenth and early twentieth centuries. More than half of these children were not "full orphans"—they had lost one parent but not both, or both parents were living but unable to take care of their children. Some children stayed in orphan asylums only a few weeks or months until their families were able to reclaim them. Many children were placed in other families in distant counties or states, with or without adoption. These records contain precious genealogical information for countless families with roots in Hamilton County: birthdates, birthplaces, birth parents, foster parents, residences, and other family details.

Types of orphan asylum records

- Admission and dismissal records
- Child and family histories
- Surrender records (parents releasing custody to the asylum)
- Indenture/placement/adoption records
- Agreements with foster families
- Visitors' observations of children in foster homes
- Reports of daily activities
- Letters
- School reports and grades
- Newspaper articles
- Board minutes with names of children

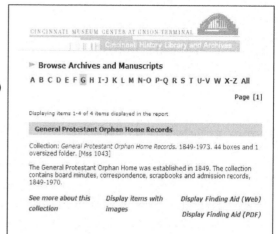

Record locations

The records of six orphan asylums are available for research at the Cincinnati History Library and Archives (CHLA), which has placed finding aids for all six (including five with children's names) on its website. On the home page, http://library.cincymuseum.org, select Archives and Manuscripts, and type in the name of the orphan asylum or pick the first letter to bring up a list of collections starting with that letter. Click Display Finding Aid and use Control-F to search for names. The CHLA collections include

- Children's Home of Cincinnati, 1864-1924, finding aid without names on CHLA's website (use steps described above); records also at the Children's Home, https://www.thechildrenshomecinti.org
- Cincinnati Orphan Asylum, 1833-1948, finding aid at http://library.cincymuseum.org/archives/mss1000-1099/Mss1053-register.pdf (partial); records in the collection of the Convalescent Home for Children (successor to the asylum), finding aid with names on CHLA's website (use steps described above)
- German General Protestant Orphan Home, 1849-1973, finding aid with names at http://library.cincymuseum.org/archives/mss1000-1099/Mss1043-register.pdf; records also at Beech Acres (successor to the asylum), https://beechacres.org
- Home for the Friendless and Foundlings, 1855-1973, records in the collection of the Maple Knoll Hospital and Home; finding aid with names at http://library.cincymuseum.org/archives/mss900-999/Mss995-register.pdf
- New Orphan Asylum for Colored Children, 1844-1967, finding aid with names at http://library.cincymuseum.org/archives/mss1000-1099/Mss1059-register.pdf
- St. Aloysius Orphan Asylum, 1837-2013, finding aid with names at http://library.cincymuseum.org/archives/mss1000-1099/Mss1098-register.pdf

The records of six asylums are available in other repositories:

- Bethany Homes for Girls, 1898-?, and Boys, 1909-1934, at the Archives of the Community of the Transfiguration, http://www.ctsisters.org
- Boys' Protectory, 1868-1972, and St. Vincent Home for Boys, 1905-1934, at the University of Notre Dame Archives, http://archives.nd.edu/findaids/ead/index/psf001.htm
- House of Refuge: 1850-1852 and 1883-1885 case files are in the Public Library of Cincinnati and Hamilton County (PLCH) Digital Library, https://digital.cincinnatilibrary.org. Records for 1869-1882 and 1891-1902 are in the Archives and Rare Books Library of the University of Cincinnati, http://digital.libraries.uc.edu/collections/refuge.
- St. Joseph Orphan Asylum, 1852 to date, at the St. Joseph Orphanage

The records of two maternity/infant homes may be in the Salvation Army Heritage Museum, https://easternusa.salvationarmy.org/use/booth-maternity-homes:

- Catherine Booth Home, 1909-1998
- Evangeline Booth Home, 1917-after 1930

The Archdiocese of Cincinnati (http://www.catholiccincinnati.org/ministries-offices/archives-office/genealogy) has the sacramental records of births, marriages and deaths that occurred in most of the Catholic asylums:

- Boys' Protectory, 1868-1972
- Our Lady of the Woods (Girls Town), 1858-1972
- St. Joseph Infant Asylum, 1873-?
- St. Vincent Home for Boys, 1905-1934
- Probably Mount St. Mary Training School, 1873-1959

Indexes

In addition to the five finding aids with names on the CHLA website, these indexes are available.

- Children's Home: "Children's Home of Cincinnati Surrender Records, 1865-1890," *The Tracer* (September 2002-June 2004), has birthdates and birthplaces, names of parents or guardians.
- Cincinnati Orphan Asylum: List of children bound from the asylum and to whom they were bound, 1835-1851, in manuscript register at CHLA.
- German General Protestant Orphan Home: Many names are indexed in *The Tracer* (February 2011-November 2011). Six sets of German records translated into English are stored with the original records at CHLA.
- House of Refuge: PLCH has indexes (not online) to the 1850-1852 and 1883-1885 case volumes which are online. 1850-1852 names are indexed in *The Tracer* (September 2014 and March 2015).
- St. Aloysius Orphan Asylum: "St. Aloysius Orphan Society," *The Tracer* (June 2018), has names of children accepted between 1837 and 1862.

Tracer articles

- "Cincinnati Orphan Asylums and Their Records, Parts One and Two," February and May 2011
- "German General Protestant Orphan Home Records, 1849-1973," February 2011
- "Records of the House of Refuge," September 2014
- "More House of Refuge Records Now Online," March 2018
- "New Finding Aid with Indexes for St. Aloysius Orphanage Records," September 2017

Tax Lists and Indexes, 1796-1838

Two types of tax records survive for Hamilton County before 1839: real property or land tax records, 1802-1838 (and a few earlier lists), and personal property tax records, 1826-1834. No Hamilton County tax records are known to exist for 1803-1805, 1815, and 1831-1832. Later records were destroyed by various courthouse fires.

Taxpayers named on real property tax lists owned the land described but could have lived anywhere. Land owners were identified in the tax lists as residents or non-residents of the county in 1801-1802, 1806-1808, and 1820-1823, and in 1824-1825 in Cincinnati Township only.

Personal property tax lists provide proof of residence, because owners of horses and other taxable items were taxed in the township where they lived. People who owned only one cow and no other taxable personal property were not taxed. All other personal property owners should be listed annually from 1826 to 1834.

This inventory summarizes the location of every known Hamilton County tax list and index. For most years, the key to searching tax lists is finding the township, since the names are primarily arranged by township beginning in 1810. The order of the 1811-1825 townships is provided in the tax list inventory. From 1826 to 1838 the order of townships is Symmes, Sycamore, Springfield, Colerain, Crosby, Whitewater, Miami, Delhi, Storrs, Green, Millcreek, Fulton, Columbia, Anderson, Cincinnati. Within the township, or in a list not separated by township, look for the pages with surnames grouped by the first letter of the surname of interest.

1801-1838 tax duplicate lists are digitized but not indexed on FamilySearch; use this list to go directly to the beginning image. Sign in at the home page, https://www.familysearch.org, move the cursor to Search, and click Catalog. Click Film/Fiche Number and enter the microfilm number provided below; click Update. Click on the resulting title: "Tax Records of Ohio, 1801-1814," "Tax Records of Various Counties, 1810," or "Duplicate Tax Records of Hamilton County, Ohio 1816-1838." Click on the camera icon to the right of the film number, type the beginning image number, and click enter to start browsing. 1827-1838 tax lists are on individual reels.

Repository abbreviations: CHLA, Cincinnati History Library and Archives; FHL, Family History Library (FamilySearch); OHC, Ohio History Connection. Search for items in CHLA's Digital Journals at http://library.cincymuseum.org/journals/journals.htm.

YEAR	TOWNSHIP	FORM	LOCATION	TYPE
1796	Columbia	List	CHLA, Mss fC726 RMV	Real
		Index	*Quarterly Publication of the Historical and Philosophical Society of Ohio* 14 (April-July 1919): 5-16, CHLA's Digital Journals	
		Index	Robert Craig, *Columbia Township, Hamilton County, Ohio, Tax List – 1796* (Cincinnati: Robert D. Craig, 1963).	
1798		List	Not in CHLA or OHC	Real
		Index	Ronald Vern Jackson, *Ohio Tax Lists, 1800-1810* (Bountiful, Utah: Accelerated Indexing Systems, 1977).	
	Miami	Index	Marjorie Byrnside Burress, *Early Rosters of Cincinnati and Hamilton County*, 61.	
	Cincinnati	Index	*Early Rosters*, 25	
1799		List	Not in CHLA or OHC	Real
	Cincinnati	Index	*Early Rosters*, 22	
1801	Anderson	List	FHL Film 522837, starting on image 7. Additions start on image 142.	Real

YEAR	TOWNSHIP	TYPE	LOCATION	TYPE
	Anderson	Index	Fay Maxwell, *Ohio's Virginia Military Tract: Index of 1801 Tax List* (Worthington, OH: Ohio Genealogy Center, 1991).	
	Anderson	Index	Esther Powell, *Early Ohio Tax Records* (Baltimore: Genealogical Publishing Co., 1985), 436.	
	Anderson	Index	*Ohio Tax Lists, 1800-1810*	
1802	Entire county	List	OHC Series 62, State Auditor's records, Box 4, Folder 15. Microfiche in Dayton Metro Library, Greene County Public Library, Montgomery County Records Center and Archives.	Real
1803-1805		List	No lists known	
1806	No township listed	List	Images 400-449 on FHL Film 522838 item 4.	Real
		Index	*Ohio Tax Lists, 1800-1810*	
1807	No township listed	List	Images 321-369 on FHL Film 522839 item 5.	Real
1808	Townships listed	List	Images 336-377 on FHL Film 522840 items 3-4.	Real
	Columbia	List	CHLA Mss qC726T RMV	
	Columbia	Index	*Bulletin of the Historical and Philosophical Society of Ohio* 17 (July 1959): 233-238, CHLA's Digital Journals	
	Columbia	Index	*The Tracer* 5:4 (September 1984), 98. Also *Early Rosters,* 55.	
	Sycamore	Index	Sycamore Township. J. G. Olden, *Historical Sketches and Early Reminiscences of Hamilton County, Ohio* (Cincinnati: H. Watkin, 1882), 161. Also *Early Rosters,* 119.	
1809	No township listed	List	Images 198-245 on FHL Film 522842 (A-N various counties).	Real
		Index	*Ohio Tax Lists, 1800-1810*	
	Springfield	Index	Springfield Township. Olden, *Historical Sketches and Early Reminiscences of Hamilton County, Ohio,* 156. Also *Early Rosters,* 114.	
1810		List	No lists known	Real
		Transcript	FHL Film 534819, starting on image 121. *Name index,* images 207-226, with page number and township.	
		Index	Gerald M. Petty, *Ohio 1810 Tax Duplicate* (Columbus, OH: 1977). *Early Rosters,* 42; *Ohio Tax Lists, 1800-1810.* Esther Powell, *Early Ohio Tax Records* (Baltimore: Genealogical Publishing Co., 1985), 153.	
		Index	"1810 Hamilton County Tax List" in USGenWeb Archives, submitted by Beth Graves; http://files.usgwarchives.net/oh/hamilton/land/taxlists/1810.txt	
1811		List	Images 430-467 on FHL Film 522843. Township order: Cincinnati, Mill Creek, Crosby, Anderson, Springfield, Sycamore, Columbia, Whitewater, Green, Miami, Colerain.	Real
	Mill Creek	Index	*Bulletin of the Historical and Philosophical Society of Ohio* 18 (April 1960): 152-157, CHLA's Digital Journals	

YEAR	TOWNSHIP	TYPE	LOCATION	TYPE
1812		List	Images 467-945 on FHL Film 514124. Township order: Cincinnati, Columbia, Mill Creek, Sycamore, Colerain, Anderson, Whitewater, Springfield, Crosby, Green, Miami (first part of Miami is omitted).	Real
	Mill Creek	Index	*Bulletin of the Historical and Philosophical Society of Ohio* 18 (July 1960): 219-221, CHLA's Digital Journals	
		Index	TLC Genealogy, *The 1812 Census of Ohio: A Statewide Index of Taxpayers* (Miami Beach, FL: 1992). Not a census.	
		Index	Name lists in *Early Rosters* for townships of Crosby, 83; Green, 92; Miami (partial), 72; Whitewater, 72.	
1813		List	Images 436-486 on FHL Film 514126. Township order: Cincinnati, Columbia, Mill Creek, Sycamore, Colerain, Anderson, Whitewater, Springfield, Crosby, Green, Miami.	Real
1814	Alphabetical townships	List	Images 100-150 on FHL Film 514129.	Real
1815			No Ohio tax lists	
1816	Alphabetical townships	List	Images 7-89 on FHL Film 559350.	Real
1817	Alphabetical townships	List	Images 97-190 on FHL Film 559350.	Real
	Cincinnati	List	CHLA, Mss fC574r RMV. Actually a valuation list and census with several information items.	
	Cincinnati	Index	Marie Dickoré, *Census for Cincinnati, Ohio, 1817: and Hamilton County, Ohio, Voters' Lists, 1798-1799* (Cincinnati: Historical and Philosophical Society of Ohio, 1960).	
1818	Alphabetical townships	List	Images 8-82 on FHL Film 506585.	Real
1819	Reverse alphabetical townships	List	FHL Film 506585, starting on image 89. The entire series was filmed and digitized backwards, from Whitewater Township to Anderson Township.	Real
1820	One list for county	List	FHL Film 506585, starting on image 166.	Real
		Index	FHL Film 1562221 Item 2. Microfilmed card file.	
1821	One list for county	List	FHL Film 506585, starting on image 257.	Real
1822	Two lists: Anderson, outside	List	FHL Film 506585. Hamilton County outside Anderson Township starts on image 359, Anderson Township starts on image 451.	Real
1823	Two lists: Anderson, outside	List	FHL Film 506585. Hamilton County outside Anderson Township starts on image 475, Anderson Township starts on image 551.	Real
1824	Cincinnati	List	FHL Film 506586, starting on image 8.	Real
1825	Cincinnati	List	FHL Film 506586, starting on image 92.	Real
		Index	Gerald M. Petty, *Index of the Ohio 1825 Tax Duplicate* (Columbus, Ohio: Petty's Press, 1981).	
1826		List	Images on FHL Film 506586 start on image 178.	Real and personal

YEAR	TOWNSHIP	TYPE	LOCATION	TYPE
1827		List	FHL Film 506587.	Real and personal
1828		List	FHL Film 506588.	Real and personal
1829		List	FHL Film 506589. See image 8 for an *index of townships* (not names) *with page numbers.*	Real and personal
1830		List	FHL Film 506590.	Real and personal
1831-1832			No Hamilton County tax lists	
1833		List	FHL Film 506591. See image 8 for an *index of townships* (not names) *with page numbers.*	Real and personal
1834		List	FHL Film 506592.	Real and personal
1835		List	FHL Film 506593.	Real
		Index	Gerald M. Petty, *Index of the Ohio 1835 Tax Duplicate* (Columbus, OH: Petty's Press, 1981).	
1836		List	FHL Film 506594.	Real
1837		List	FHL Film 506595.	Real
1838		List	FHL Film 506596.	Real

For detailed information and research strategies, see these articles in the March 2016 issue of *The Tracer:*

- "Using 1801-1838 Hamilton County, Ohio, Tax Records: A Case Study"
- "Research in Hamilton County Property Tax Records"
- "Inventory of Hamilton County Tax Lists and Indexes, 1796-1838"
- "Access to Hamilton County Tax Records Online"

1830 tax list

Vital Records

OFFICE	ADDRESS	DATES	FORMAT	PLACE/HOURS
City of Cincinnati Elm Street Health Center	1525 Elm St. Cincinnati, OH 45202 (513)352-1493 www.cincinnati-oh.gov/health	Births: Dec. 1908-present Deaths: Dec. 1908-present	Books and microfilm	Research by appt. only, 4th floor T-TH: 9-11 a.m. & 2-4 p.m.
Norwood Health Center	2059 Sherman Ave. Cincinnati, OH 45212 (513) 458-4600 www.norwoodhealth.org	Births & Deaths Mostly after 1908		M-F: 8-5 p.m. Call for appointment
Cities of Reading and St. Bernard	250 Wm Howard Taft Cincinnati, OH 45219 (513) 946-7805	Births & Deaths: 1909-present 1889-present		Records at Hamilton County General Health District
Hamilton County General Health District	250 Wm Howard Taft Cincinnati, OH 45219 (513) 946-7805 www.hamiltoncountyhealth.org HCPHCustServ@hamilton-co.org	Births 1875-present Deaths 1891-present not including Cincinnati and Norwood	File Cards	No appointment needed except for multiple records M-W & F 7:30-4:30 TH: 8:30-4:30 p.m.

Researchers may use cameras and smart phones (and scanners, in some offices) to photograph non-certified Ohio birth and death records, free of charge.

Cincinnati office: Records of births in Cincinnati and other Ohio jurisdictions, 1909 to the present, and deaths in Cincinnati only, 1909 to the present.

Norwood office: Records of births and deaths in Norwood and other Ohio jurisdictions, 1909 to the present.

Hamilton County office: Records of births in Hamilton County outside Cincinnati and Norwood, 1875-1908; births in Hamilton County and other Ohio jurisdictions, 1909 to the present; and deaths in Hamilton County outside Cincinnati and Norwood, 1891 to the present.

Online records

- 1874-1908 Cincinnati births and 1865-1908 Cincinnati deaths, http://digitalprojects.libraries.uc.edu/Births_and_Deaths
- 1863-1908 births and 1881-1908 deaths registered in Hamilton County Probate Court, www.familysearch.org and www.probatect.org
- Delayed births, 1941-1963 (recording period, not period of births), www.familysearch.org; 1968-1973 recording period, www.probatect.org
- 1909-1953 Ohio deaths, www.familysearch.org

For details and more links, see these HCGS web pages: Births and Baptisms; Death Records.

Also see "Hamilton County, Ohio, Vital Records" in the March 2006 issue of *The Tracer*. While ordering and online information has changed since then, the historical information and alternative sources are still useful.

Chapter 6: Local Resources

Hamilton County Resources

NAME	ADDRESS	DATES & INFORMATION	PLACE/HOURS
Archives and Rare Books Library	University of Cincinnati Carl Blegen Library P.O. Box 210113 Cincinnati, OH 45221 (513)556-1959 https://libraries.uc.edu/arb.html	Ohio Network Collection Cinti. Births 1874-1908 Cinti. Deaths 1865-1908 Citizenship 1837-1916 Wills 1791-1901 See list on pages 8-9	8th Floor M-F: 8-5 p.m.
LDS Family History Center (Norwood)	Cincinnati Stake 5505 Bosworth Pl. Norwood, OH 45212 (513)531-5624	Many microfilms on long-term loan, including German church records and others	W-TH-SA: 10-2 p.m. T-TH: 6-9 p.m.
LDS Family History Center (Montgomery)	Cincinnati North Stake 8250 Cornell Rd. Cincinnati, OH 45249 (513)489-3036	(Does not receive mail)	T-TH-SA: 10-2 p.m. T-TH: 6-9 p.m.
The Cincinnati History Library and Archives Founded in 1831	The Museum Center Cincinnati Union Terminal 1301 Western Ave. Cincinnati, OH 45203 (513)287-7030 http://library.cincymuseum.org	Manuscript holdings Map collection Vital Statistics File Extensive photographs City & county directories See pages 6-7	M-F: 12-5 p.m. SA: 10-5 p.m.
US District Court of Southern Ohio	Potter Stewart U.S. Courthouse 550 Main St. (at Fifth St.) Cincinnati, OH 45202 Office of Clerk: (513)564-7500	Naturalizations Index 1800s-1990 (records in Chicago National Archives) Records 1956-1990	Room 324
American Jewish Archives	Hebrew Union College 3101 Clifton Ave. Cincinnati, OH 45220 (513)221-1875 www.americanjewisharchives.org	Extensive collections on American Jewish ancestry; write for outline of genealogical resources	M-Th: 9-5 p.m. F: 9-3 p.m.
Archives of the Archdiocese of Cincinnati (Catholic Churches)	100 E. Eighth Street Cincinnati, OH 45202 www.catholiccincinnati.org	19 counties in SW Ohio: Baptisms, Confirmations, Marriages, and Funerals (written requests only) See details on pages 57-59	Must complete request form on website
Episcopal Archives	Episcopal Diocese of Southern Ohio 412 Sycamore St. Cincinnati, OH 45202 (513)421-0311 www.diosohio.org	See details on page 33	M-F: 9-5 p.m.

NAME	ADDRESS	DATES & INFORMATION	PLACE/HOURS
Presbytery of Cincinnati	1323 Myrtle Ave. Cincinnati, OH 45206 (513)221-4850 www.presbyteryofcincinnati.org	Records for early or closed churches are in Philadelphia, PA or at the Cincinnati History Library & Archives	M-F: 8:30-4:30 p.m.
German Heritage Museum	4764 West Fork Road (513)598-5732 www.gacl.org/museum	German American Citizens' League records, local German history, German family and genealogical books	May-October SU: 1-5 p.m. or by appt.
Holocaust & Humanity Center	Nancy and David Wolf Holocaust & Humanity Center 1301 Western Ave, Suite 2101 (513)497-3055 www.holocaustandhumanity.org	Library and archives	Museum hours: M-TH: 8:30-5 p.m. F: 8:30-4 p.m. SU: 11-3 p.m.
Irish Heritage Center of Cincinnati	3905 Eastern Ave. Cincinnati, OH 45226 (513)533-0100 www.irishcenterofcincinnati.com	Library	By appt.
Cincinnati Fire Museum	315 W. Court Street #1 Cincinnati, OH 45202 (513)621-5553 www.cincyfiremuseum.com		Museum T-SA: 10-4 p.m.
Greater Cincinnati Police Museum	308 Reading Road, Suite 201 Cincinnati, OH 45202 (513)300-3664 www.police-museum.org		Museum T, TH, SA: 10-4 p.m.
Longview State Hospital		Cemetery list – 1924-1967 PLCH and *The Tracer*	
St. Aloysius Orphanage Founded in 1832	4721 Reading Rd. Cincinnati, OH 45237 (513)242-7600	See pages 62-63	M-F: 8-5 p.m.
Beech Acres (General Protestant Orphan Home) Founded in 1849	6881 Beechmont Ave. Cincinnati, OH 45230 (513)231-6630 www.beechacres.org	See pages 62-63	M-F: 8-5 p.m.
St. Joseph Orphanage Founded in 1829	5400 Edalbert Dr. Cincinnati, OH 45239 (513)741-3100 www.sjokids.org	(Written requests only)	M-F: 8:30-5 p.m.
The Children's Home of Cincinnati Founded in 1864	5050 Madison Rd. Cincinnati, OH 45227 (513)272-2800 www.thechildrenshomecinti.org	Indexed in *The Tracer;* see pages 62-63	M-F: 8-4:30 p.m.

Hamilton County Historical Societies

NAME	ADDRESS	DATES & INFORMATION	PLACE/HOURS
Addyston Historical Society	235 Main St. Addyston, OH 45001 (513)941-1313	www.addystonohio.org	
Anderson Twp. Historical Society	6550 Clough Pike Cincinnati, OH 45244 Mail to: P.O. Box 30174 Cincinnati, OH 45230 (513)231-2114	www.andersontownshiphistoric alsociety.org Extensive collection of records on families and history *Tracer,* December 2017	Research Library: by appt. Log House: 1st & 3rd SU: 1-4 (Jun-Oct)
Blue Ash Historical Society	Hunt House Museum 4364 Hunt Road Cincinnati, OH 45241 (513)324-7145	blueashhistoric@gmail.com	Hunt House Museum
Cheviot Historical Society	3814 Harrison Ave. Cincinnati, OH 45211 (513)662-9615		
Coleraine Historical Society	P.O. Box 53726 Cincinnati, OH 45251 (513)385-7566	www.colerainehistorical-oh.org Museum, 4725 Springdale *Tracer,* June 2017	2nd & 4th SA: 10-2 p.m. Or by appt.
College Hill Historical Society	1422 Hillcrest Rd. Cincinnati, OH 45224	collegehillhistory@gmail.com	
Crosby Township Historical Society	8910 Wiley Road Harrison, OH 45030 (513)367-2186	www.crosbytwp.org	
Delhi Historical Society	468 Anderson Ferry Rd. Cincinnati, OH 45238 (513)451-4313	www.delhihistoricalsociety.org *Tracer,* December 2016	Farmhouse SU,T,TH: 12:30-3 Research by appt. only
Glendale Heritage Preservation	44 Village Square Cincinnati, OH 45246 (513)771-8722	www.glendaleheritage.org	Museum TH & SA: 11-3
Green Township Historical Assn.	3973 Grace Ave. Cincinnati, OH 45211 (513)574-9909	www.greentwphistory.com	
Greenhills Historical Society	8 Enfield St. Cincinnati, OH 45218 (513)703-2970	greenhillshistory@gmail.com	
Harrison Village Historical Society	P.O. Box 419 6590 Kilby Road Harrison, OH 45030 (513)367-9285	Open by appt. only	Looker Home 10580 Marvin Rd.
Indian Hill Historical Society	8560 Camargo Road Cincinnati, OH 45243 (513)891-1873	www.indianhill.org Array of village information at the Resource Center/Library – Buchingham Lodge; *Tracer,* March 2019	Buchingham Lodge 8650 Camargo Rd. M-F: 10-5

NAME	ADDRESS	DATES & INFORMATION	PLACE/HOURS
Lockland Historical Society	304 Westview Cincinnati, OH 45215 (513)563-6942	Open by appt.	
(Greater) Loveland Historical Society	201 Riverside Dr. Loveland, OH 45140 (513)683-5692	www.lovelandmuseum.org	Museum & Research Library SA-SU: 1-4
Madeira Historical Society	7226 Miami Ave. Madeira, OH 45243 (513)561-9069	www.maderiahs.org Museum and headquarters in the historic Miller House, a Sears catalog home, 1922. *Tracer*, September 2018	Miller House Museum 1st SA & 3rd SU: 1-4 Tours by appt.
Mariemont Preservation Foundation	3919 Plainville Rd. Cincinnati, OH 45227 (513)272-1166	www.mariemontpreservation.org	Archives SA: 9-12 p.m.
Miami Historical Society of Whitewater Twp.	7998 Main Street Box 8 Miamitown, OH 45041	www.miamihistoricalsociety.com	Historic Town Hall
Montgomery Historical Preservation Assoc.	7650 Cooper Rd. Cincinnati, OH 45242 (513)891-2424 (City Hall) (513)984-1465	www.montgomeryohio.org/about	Wilder-Swaim House
Mt. Healthy Historical Society	1546 McMakin Ave. Cincinnati, OH 45231 (513)522-3939	www.mthealthyhistory.org Tours and research by appt. only	Museum SA: 9-11 a.m. 1st SU: 1-3 p.m.
Norwood Historical Society	4121 Forest Ave. Cincinnati, OH 45212 (513)741-7951 norwoodhistory@hotmail.com	www.norwoodhistoricalsociety.org	
Price Hill Historical Society	3640 Warsaw Ave. Cincinnati, OH 45205 (513)251-2888	www.pricehill.org Exhibits, displays, photographs, and information on families, buildings, businesses, schools and churches	T & TH: 1-4 p.m. or by appt.
Reading Historical Society	22 W. Benson St. Cincinnati, OH 45215 (513)733-2787	www.readingohio.org	
Sayler Park Historical Society	(513)673-3368	www.saylerpark.org/sayler-park-historical-society	
St. Bernard/Ludlow Grove Historical Society	110 Washington Ave. Cincinnati, OH 45217 (513)242-7770	www.stbernardhistory.org	
Society of Historic Sharonville	11115 Main Street Cincinnati, OH 45241 (513)563-9756	www.sharonville.org/historic society.aspx Extensive file collection about area residents, buildings and other places in the greater Cincinnati area	Museum: Creek & Main Sts. SU: 12-4 p.m. or by appt.

NAME	ADDRESS	DATES & INFORMATION	PLACE/HOURS
Symmes Township Historical Society	P.O. Box 498917 (513)683-6644 Cincinnati, OH 45249	www.symmeshistoricalsociety.com	
Terrace Park Historical Society	100 Miami Ave. Terrace Park, OH 45174 (513)248-1777	www.tphistoricalsociety.org *Tracer* article on Terrace Park Building Survey website, August 2010	Office Open: TH: 1-6 p.m. or by appt.
Three Rivers Historical Society	112 S. Miami Ave. Cleves, OH 45002		
Westwood Historical Society	PO Box 11095 Cincinnati, OH 45211	www.westwoodhistorical.org	
Wyoming Historical Society	800 Oak St. Cincinnati, OH 45215 (513)842-1383	www.wyominghistorical.com	T: 10:30-3 p.m. or by appt.

HCGS Cemeteries Web Page

These lists and links are on the HCGS Cemeteries web page, https://hcgsohio.org/cpage.php?pt=63:

- A master list of all former and present Hamilton County burial sites, arranged by township, with the year of first recording, location, size, name changes, and present status (formerly published in *A Guide*)
- A list of 180 cemeteries indexed in *Hamilton County, Ohio, Burial Records*, a series of 22 volumes
- A list of cemeteries indexed in *The Tracer*
- Indexes to cemetery lot deeds

The web page also contains details and links to indexes for the Veteran Burials Project. In 2013 many HCGS volunteers started a project to document Civil War soldiers buried in Hamilton County cemeteries. A link to a comprehensive list of these soldiers is on the Cemeteries web page. Volunteers also photographed grave markers, when found, and these photos have been uploaded to their Find A Grave memorials.

Subsequent volunteer projects have documented veteran burials from all wars prior to World War II. A project to document World War I veterans was completed in 2019. Check the website for the most recent updated lists and information.

GRAVES REGISTRATION CARD HAMILTON COUNTY CINCINNATI, OHIO

Name HUENEFELD, HENRY
Address 4162 Witler Street Cincinnati
Date of Death April 8, 1922 Place Cincinnati
Cause Septic cystitis Date of Burial April 11, 1922
Date of Birth September 17, 1841 Place Oldenberg, Germany
Name of Cemetery Vine Street Hill Location 3703 Vine Street
Lot No. 113 Section No. 2 Block No. -- Grave No. 7
Marker: Flat X Upright None
Next of Kin Wife: Caroline Huenefeld, 4162 Witler
(Name)
(E)
SERVICE RECORD Columbus GAR Records
Ham. Co. Comm. Records
Soldiers & Sailors Relief
War Served In: Civil
Date Enlisted May 2, 1864 Date Discharged No record Serial No. --
Branch of Service Army Rank Private
Company, Outfit or Ship 165th BN O.V.I. CO A.

Active Cemeteries

Many active cemeteries have been indexed as noted, and the indexes are available at the Public Library of Cincinnati and Hamilton County. See the list of published *Hamilton County, Ohio, Burial Records* on page 16.

CEMETERY	ESTABLISHED	ADDRESS	COMMENTS
Archdiocese of Cincinnati Cemetery Office (Cincinnati Catholic Cemetery Society)		11000 Montgomery Rd. Cincinnati, OH 45249 (513)489-0300 www.cccsohio.org	See additional information on page 27
Arlington Memorial Gardens	1938	2145 Compton Rd. Cincinnati, OH 45231 (513)521-7003	Sectional plat listed in Springfield Twp. Book, Vol. 7
Armstrong Chapel (Predominantly Methodist)	1830	5125 Drake Rd. Cincinnati, OH 45243 (513)561-4220	Indexed in Columbia Twp. Cemetery Book, Vol. 11
Baltimore Pike (Predominantly German Protestant)	1884	3200 Costello Ave. Cincinnati, OH 45211 (513)921-1216	On microfilm at PLCH* Indexed in Baltimore Pike Cemetery Book, Vol. 21
Beech Grove (Predominantly African-American)	1889	436 Fleming Rd. Cincinnati, OH 45231 (513)931-2629	Indexed in Springfield Twp. Cemetery Book, Vol. 7
Bridgetown (Predominantly Protestant)	1865	4337 Harrison Ave. Cincinnati, OH 45211 (513)574-0360	Indexed in Green Twp. Cemetery Book, Vol. 10
Calvary Cemetery (Originally from St. Francis De Sales Church) (Predominantly Catholic)	1849	1721 Duck Creek Rd. Cincinnati, OH 45207 (513)961-2179	Indexed in Calvary Cemetery Book, Vol. 12
Crown Hill Memorial Park	1970	11825 Pippin Rd. Cincinnati, OH 45231 (513)851-7170	Burial cards on file in office
Flagspring (I.O.O.F.) (Cemetery located on Roundbottom Road near Ohio Rt. 32 in Newtown)	1863	c/o Village of Newtown 3536 Church St. Newtown, OH 45244 (513)561-2300	Indexed in Anderson Twp. Cemetery Book, Vol. 2
Gate of Heaven (Predominantly Catholic)	1947	11000 Montgomery Rd. Cincinnati, OH 45249 (513)489-0300	www.gateofheaven.org Burials online: Locate a Loved One
Glen Haven Cemetery located Madison & New Biddinger Rds.	1890	213 Elbern Ave. Harrison, OH 45030 (513)367-6541	Indexed in Harrison Twp. Cemetery Book, Vol. 14
Guardian Angels (Predominantly Catholic)	1904	6536 Beechmont Ave. Cincinnati, OH 45230 (513)231-7440	Indexed in Anderson Twp. Cemetery Book, Vol. 2
Hopewell (Predominantly Protestant)	By 1811	10205 Montgomery Rd. Cincinnati, OH 45246 (513)791-8292	Indexed in Sycamore Twp. Cemetery Book, Vol. 8 www.hopewellmontgomery.cemsites.com

CEMETERY	ESTABLISHED	ADDRESS	COMMENTS
Indian Hill Episcopal-Presbyterian	1952	6000 Drake Rd. Cincinnati, OH 45243 (513)561-6805	Indexed in Columbia Twp. Cemetery Book, Vol. 11
Jewish Cemeteries of Greater Cincinnati: Covedale (O) Golf Manor #1 Golf Manor #2 Golf Manor #3 Beth Hamedrash Hagodol Beth Jacob/Price Hill American Beneficial Tiferath Israel Yad Chorutzim New Hope Kneseth Israel Northern Hills (C)	1923 1900 1922 1913 1916 1916 1939 1922 1912	2111 Anderson Ferry Rd. 5350 and 5375 Sidney Rd. Cincinnati, Ohio 45238 (513)961-0178	Online index: www.jcemcin.org/genealogy-2 (O) = Orthodox (C) = Conservative (R) = Reform
Jewish Cemeteries of Greater Cincinnati - Price Hill Love Brothers (C) United Jewish (R) Judah Touro (R) Montefiore (R) Beth Tefyla/Schachnus (O) Hirsh Hoffert (O) Chesed Chel Emes (O) Adath Israel (C)	1919 1862 1856 1871 1874 1920 1921 1855	1619 Rosemont Ave. 1657 Rosemont Ave. 1675 Sunset Ave. 1711 Sunset Ave. 1405 Sunset Ave. 1661 Sunset Ave. Cincinnati, OH 45238 (513)961-0178	Online index: www.jcemcin.org/genealogy-2 (O) = Orthodox (C) = Conservative (R) = Reform
Jewish Cemeteries of Greater Cincinnati - United Jewish Cemeteries Walnut Hills (R) Clifton (R) Price Hill (R) Montgomery (R/C) Loveland	1850 1848 1862 1970s 2017	Office: (513)961-0178 3400 Montgomery Rd Cincinnati, OH 45207 3400 Montgomery Rd. 730 Ludlow Ave. 1657 Rosemont Ave. 7885 Ivygate Ln. 712 Loveland-Miamiville Rd.	Online index: www.jcemcin.org/genealogy-2 (O) = Orthodox (C) = Conservative (R) = Reform
Landmark Memorial Gardens	1977	500 Oak Rd. Cincinnati, OH 45246 (513)771-4460	
Laurel (I.O.O.F.)	1863	5915 Roe Cincinnati, OH 45227 (513)271-0104	Indexed in Columbia Twp. Cemetery Book, Vol. 11
Laurel Memorial Gardens	ca. 1926	10010 Humphrey Rd. Cincinnati, OH 45242 (513)791-0436	

CEMETERY	ESTABLISHED	ADDRESS	COMMENTS
Maple Grove (Located on Valley Junction Rd.)	1884	112 S. Miami Ave. Cleves, OH 45002 (513)941-2466	Indexed in Miami Twp. Cemetery Book, Vol. 4
Mt. Washington	1855	P.O. Box 30025 Cincinnati, OH 45230	Indexed in Anderson Twp. Cemetery Book, Vol. 2 www.cemeteryindex.com /mtwashington1
Oak Hill	1911	11200 Princeton Rd. Cincinnati, OH 34246 (513)771-7681	Indexed in Springfield Twp. Cemetery Book, Vol. 7 www.springgrove.org
Pleasant Ridge (Predominantly Presbyterian)	1790	5950 Montgomery Rd. Cincinnati, OH 45213 (513)631-9707	Indexed in Columbia Twp. Cemetery Book, Vol. 11
Reading Cemetery Assn. (Predominantly Protestant)	ca. 1802	200 W. Columbia Ave. Cincinnati, OH 45215 (513)554-1027	Indexed in Sycamore Twp. Cemetery Book, Vol. 8 Burial cards in office
Rest Haven Memorial Park	1929	10209 Plainfield Cincinnati, OH 45242 (513) 563-2260	Sectional Plats in Sycamore Twp. Cemetery Book, Vol. 8; burials, www.resthavenmemorialpark.com
St. Aloysius Gonzaga Church (Predominantly Catholic)	1866	4366 Bridgetown Rd. Cincinnati, OH 45211 (513)574-4840	Parish Cemetery Only Indexed in Green Twp Cemetery Book, Vol. 10
St. Bernard, Taylor Creek (Predominantly Catholic)	1867	7130 Springdale Rd. Cincinnati, OH 45247 (513)353-4207	Indexed in Colerain Twp. Cemetery Book, Vol. 6
St. James (earlier called St. Jacob) (Predominantly Catholic)	1844	3565 Hubble Rd. Cincinnati, OH 45247 (513)741-5300	Indexed in Green Twp. Cemetery Book, Vol. 10
St. John (Predominantly German Catholic)	1849	4423 Vine St. Cincinnati, OH 45217 (513)242-4191	On Microfilm at PLCH* Indexed in Old St. John German Cemetery Book, Vol. 20
St. John the Baptist (Predominantly Catholic)	1859	110 N. Hill St. Harrison, OH 45030 (513)367-9086	Indexed in Harrison Twp. Cemetery Book, Vol. 14
St. John the Baptist (Predominantly Catholic)	1860	5361 Dry Ridge Rd. Cincinnati, OH 45252 (513)385-8010	Indexed in Colerain Twp. Cemetery Book, Vol. 6
St. Joseph – Old (Predominantly German Catholic)	1843	3819 W. 8th St. Cincinnati, OH 45205 (513)921-3050	On Microfilm at PLCH* Indexed in Old St. Joseph German Cemetery Book, Vol. 19 www.cccsohio.org/StJoseph
St. Joseph – New (Predominantly Irish Catholic)	1854	Pedretti & Foley Cincinnati, OH 45238 (513)251-3110	On Microfilm at PLCH* Indexed in New St. Joseph Irish Cemetery Book, Vol. 18 www.stjoenew.com - Search
St. Mary Cemetery & Mausoleum (Predominantly German Catholic)	1873	701 E. Ross Ave. Cincinnati, OH 45217 (513)242-4191	On Microfilm at PLCH*

CEMETERY	ESTABLISHED	ADDRESS	COMMENTS
St. Peter & Paul (Predominantly Catholic)	1858 (old) 1880 (new)	9412 Reading Rd. Cincinnati, OH 45215 (513)733-5445	Indexed in Sycamore Twp. Cemetery Book, Vol. 8
Spring Grove & Arboretum (second largest cemetery in U.S.)	1845	4521 Spring Grove Ave. Cincinnati, OH 45232 (513)681-6680	Images of card file on website, Locate a Loved One www.springgrove.org
Union	1825	9323 Union Cemetery Rd. Symmes Twp. OH 45140 (513)683-6644	Office also covers Kerr and Waldschmidt Cemeteries. Indexed in Symmes Township Cemeteries Book, Vol. 20
Union Baptist (Predominantly African American)	1865	4933 Cleves-Warsaw Pk. Cincinnati, OH 45238 (513)921-0452	Indexed in Union Baptist Cemetery Book, Vol. 9
United Afro-American (Colored American) on Duck Creek Road	1865	Union Baptist Church 405 W. Seventh St. Cincinnati, OH 45202 (513)381-3858	Indexed in Columbia Twp. Cemetery Book, Vol. 11
Vine Street Hill (German Evangelical Protestant Cemetery)	1849	3701 Vine St. Cincinnati, OH 45220 (513)281-1035	Indexed in Vine Street Hill Cemetery Book, Vol. 3 Cards on file in office
Walnut Hills (Predominantly German Protestant)	1843	3117 Victory Pkwy. Cincinnati, OH 45206 (513)961-1424	Indexed in Walnut Hills Cemetery Book, Vol. 16 (1843-1993) and online, www.walnuthillscemetery.org
Wesleyan (Predominantly Methodist Episcopal)	1842	4003 Colerain Ave. Cincinnati, OH 45223 (513)541-2635	Indexed in Wesleyan Cemetery Book, Vol. 1 (1842-1971) www.rootsweb.com/~ohhamcem

Public Library of Cincinnati and Hamilton County (PLCH)*

In 1812 Cincinnati had a population of 2,000. Benson Lossing, The Pictorial Field-Book of the War of 1812 *(Harper & Brothers, Publishers, 1868), 476.*

VIEW OF CINCINNATI FROM NEWPORT IN 1812.[2]

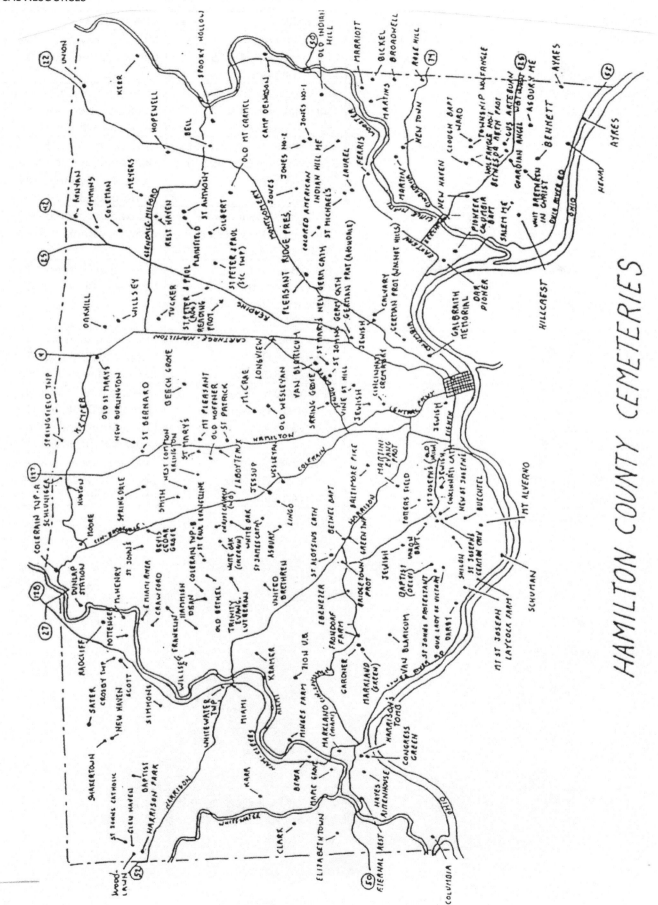

HAMILTON COUNTY CEMETERIES

Nearby Resources

STATE	PLACE/ADDRESS	COMMENTS
OHIO	Ohio Genealogical Society 611 State Route 97 West Bellville, OH 44813-8813 (419)886-1903 www.ogs.org	Library hours: T-SA: 9-5 p.m. Free for OGS members
	Ohio Department of Health Bureau of Vital Statistics P.O. Box 15098 35 E. Chestnut St. (6th floor) Columbus, OH 43215-0098 (614)466-2531	Hours: M-F: 8-5 p.m. Births from Dec. 1908 Deaths from Jan. 1964 https://odh.ohio.gov/wps/portal/gov/odh/know-our-programs/vital-statistics/vital-statistics
	Ohio History Connection Archives & Library 800 E. 17th Ave. (I-71 & 17th Ave.) Columbus, OH 43211-2474 (614)297-2510 Library, (614)297-2300 Information www.ohiohistory.org	Library Hours: W-SA: 10-5 p.m. Index of Deaths, Dec. 1908-1954 1913-1944 at www.ohiohistory.org/dindex/search.cfm
	State Library of Ohio 274 E. First Ave. Columbus, OH 43201 (614)644-7061 www.library.ohio.gov	Hours: M-F: 8-5 p.m. All genealogy material has been transferred to the Columbus Metropolitan Library
	Columbus Metropolitan Library 96 S. Grant Ave. Columbus, OH 43215 (614)645-2275 www.columbuslibrary.org	Hours: M-TH: 9-9 p.m. F-SA: 9-6 p.m., SU: 1-5 p.m. Has collections of State Library of Ohio, Palatines to America, Ohio Huguenot Society, Franklin County Genealogical Society
	Rutherford B. Hayes Presidential Center Library Spiegel Grove (corner of Hayes and Buckland Avenues) Fremont, OH 43420 (419)332-2081	Hours: M-SA: 9-5 p.m. Closed Mondays, Jan/Feb/Mar
Butler County	Butler County Records Center and Archives 123 North Third Street Hamilton, OH 45011 (513)887-3437 www.butlercountyohio.org/records	Hours: Call for appointment Marriages/Wills 1803-2003 Birth/Death 1867-1908 later records at Butler County Courthouse
	Butler County Genealogical Society P.O. Box 13006 Hamilton, OH 45013 www.butlercountyogs.org	
	Cummins Room, Lane Public Library 300 North Third St. (at Buckeye) Hamilton, OH 45011 (513)894-7156 www.lanepl.org	Hours: T 10-12 p.m., W 3-5 p.m. Ask for access in Children's Department on 2nd floor

STATE	PLACE/ADDRESS	COMMENTS
OHIO Butler County	Butler County Health Department 301 South Third St. Hamilton, OH 45011 (513)863-1771	
	Butler County Historical Society 327 N. Second St. Hamilton, OH 45011 (513)896-9930	Hours: T, TH & F: 10-3 p.m. SA 10-1 p.m.
	Midpointe Public Library 125 S. Broad St., Middletown, OH 45044 (513)424-1251 www.midpointelibrary.org	Hours: M-TH: 9-9 p.m.; F: 9-7 p.m. SA: 9-5 p.m. Emphasis on local area, colonial states, WV, KY
	Smith Library of Regional History, The Lane Libraries 441 S. Locust St., Oxford, OH 45056 (513)523-3035 www.lanepl.org/research/smith-library	Hours: M & W-F: 10-12 & 1-5 p.m. TU: 10-12 & 1-8 p.m. SA: 10-1 p.m. City of Oxford and surrounding townships, Butler County, and southwestern OH
Clermont County	Clermont County Probate Court 2379 Clermont Center Dr., Batavia, OH 45103 (513)732-7243 www.probatejuvenile.clermontcountyohio.gov	
	Clermont County Genealogical Society P.O. Box 394 Batavia, OH 45103-0394 Voice Mail: (513)723-3423 www.rootsweb.ancestry.com/~ohclecgs	Holdings at the Clermont County Public Library in Batavia, OH
	Clermont County Public Library – Doris Wood Branch 180 S. Third St. Batavia, OH 45103 (513)732-2128 www.clermontlibrary.org	Hours: M-TU: 12-8 p.m., W-TH: 10-6 p.m. F & SA: 9-5:00 p.m. Holdings of the Clermont County Genealogical Society
Warren County	Warren County Courthouse (Probate Court) 570 Justice Dr. Lebanon, OH 45036-0296 (513)932-4040	Recorder's Office, 406 Justice Dr. Health Dept., 416 S. East St.
	Warren County Historical Society 105 S. Broadway Lebanon, OH 45036 (513)932-1817 - www.wchsmuseum.org	Hours: TU-SA: 10-4 p.m.
	Warren County Genealogical Society 406 Justice Dr. Lebanon, OH 45036-2349 (513)695-1144 www.co.warren.oh.us/genealogy/index.htm	Hours: M-F: 9-4 p.m. Research center on lower level of Warren County Administration Building, Lebanon, OH
Greene County	Greene County Room, Xenia Community Library 76 E. Market Street Xenia, OH 45385 (937)352-4000 https://greenelibrary.info/locations/G	Hours: M-TH: 10-8 p.m. F: 10-6 p.m. SA: 10-5 p.m. SU: 1-5 p.m. (Sep to May only)

OHIO Highland County	SOGS Research Library, Southern State Community College 100 Hobart Drive Hillsboro, OH 45133 (800)628-7722 ext. 2680 www.sogs.info/sogs-research-library	Spring/Fall Semesters: M-TH: 8-8 p.m., F: 8-4 p.m. Summer Hours: M-TH: 8-6 p.m. F: 9-4 p.m. Class Breaks: M-F: 8-4 p.m.
KENTUCKY	Vital Statistics - State Department of Health 275 East Main St. Frankfort, KY 40621-0001 (502)564-4212	Births & Deaths from Jan. 1911 Marriage & Divorce Records from June 1958. (Available at Kenton County Library: 1911-1986)
	Kentucky State Archives 300 Coffee Tree Road Frankfort, KY 40601 (502)564-8300 https://kdla.ky.gov	Hours: M-F: 9-4 p.m.
	Martin F. Schmidt Research Library at the Kentucky History Center & Museums (Kentucky Historical Society) 100 West Broadway Frankfort, KY 40601 (502)564-1792 www.history.ky.gov	Hours: W-SA: 10-5 p.m. Library admission: $8 (free for members)
Boone County	Boone County Courthouse 2950 Washington Burlington, KY 41005 (859)334-2200 www.boonecountyky.org	
	Boone County Public Library 1786 Burlington Pike Burlington, KY 41005 (859)342-2665 www.bcpl.org	Hours: M-F: 9-9 p.m. SA: 9-5 p.m. SU: 1-5 p.m.
Campbell County	Campbell County Administration Building 1098 Monmouth St. Room 205 Newport, KY 41071 (859)292-3885 (Marriages) & (859)292-3845 (Land Records)	Hours: M-F: 8:30-4 p.m. Deeds, Wills, Mortgages, and Marriages
	(Old) Campbell County Courthouse 19 East Main St. Alexandria, KY 41011 (859)635-2151 (Records Room)	Earlier Courthouse in Alexandria, KY. Covered all of Kenton County & Campbell County, KY to 1840
	Campbell County Public Library 901 E Sixth St. Newport, KY 41071 (859)572-5035 www.cc-pl.org	Hours: M-TH: 9-9 p.m. F: 9-7 p.m. SA: 9-5 p.m. SU: 1-5 p.m.
	Campbell County Historical & Genealogical Society 19 East Main St. Alexandria, KY 41001 (859)635-6407	Hours: T: 12-8 p.m. SA: 10-3 p.m.

STATE	PLACE/ADDRESS	COMMENTS
KENTUCKY Kenton County	Kenton County Courthouses: Third & Court St.　　　5247 Madison Pk. Covington, KY 41011　　Independence KY 41051 (859)491-0702　　　(859)356-9272	Various records available 1874 to present. Earlier Courthouse in Independence, 1840 to 1874
	Kenton County Public Library Fifth & Scott Sts. Covington, KY 41011 (859)491-7610 www.kenton.lib.ky.us	Hours: M-TH: 9-9 p.m. F: 9-6 p.m. SA: 10-5 p.m. SU: 1-5 p.m.
INDIANA	Indiana State Dept. of Health Division of Vital Statistics P.O. Box 7125 Indianapolis, IN 46206-7125 (317)233-2700	Hours: M-F: 8:15-4:45 p.m. Births from Oct. 1907 (compliance by 1917) Deaths from 1900
	Dearborn County Courthouse 215B W. High St. Lawrenceburg, IN 47025 (812)537-1040 www.dearborncounty.org	
	Lawrenceburg Public Library 150 Mary St. Lawrenceburg, IN 47025 (812)537-2775 www.lpld.lib.in.us	Hours: M-TH: 9-8 p.m. F: 9-5 p.m. SA: 10-5 p.m. Research for Dearborn and contiguous IN counties
	Allen County Public Library 900 Library Plaza Ft. Wayne, IN 46802 (260)421-120 www.acpl.lib.in.us	Hours: M-TH: 9-9 p.m. F-SA: 9-6 p.m. SU: 12-5 p.m. during school year
ILLINOIS	National Archives-Great Lakes Region 7358 S. Pulaski Rd. Chicago, IL 60629 (773)581-7816	Regional archives for OH, IN, IL, MI, MN, and WS - federal records only

A view of Cincinnati in 1841, from one of the surrounding hills to the north. In the foreground is the Miami and Erie Canal, and in the distance is the Ohio River and Kentucky. Klauprech and Menzel, printer of plates (Wikipedia Commons).

Chapter 7: Online Resources

The Hamilton County Genealogical Society's Website

The Hamilton County Genealogical Society (HCGS) maintains a website that includes indexes of genealogical records (some public and some for members-only), links to public databases of Hamilton County records, explanations of how to locate and use records, videos (some public and some members-only), a calendar of genealogy programs, and information relating to unique interest groups. Members also have digital access to the *Tracer,* a quarterly publication.

The web address is https://hcgsohio.org/index.php. The content is accessed via the menu on the left side of the home page. Content is continually updated and expanded.

Databases available

Databases Available, linked from the HCGS home page, provides easy access to every database (both public and members-only) on the HCGS website.

Public databases

- Pre-Civil War veterans burials
- Index of Civil War veterans burials in Hamilton County
- Index of Service 1865-1917 veterans burials
- WPA Veteran Grave Cards (Revolutionary War—Vietnam)
- Index to *Der Christliche Apologete* 1839-1899 (abbreviated index)
- Index to Church Deaths 1890-1899 (abbreviated index)
- Index to Cemetery Lot Documents, 1859-1934
- Index to Death Notices, 1827-1910 (abbreviated index)
- Index to Ford's *History of Cincinnati*
- Index to Hamilton County Pioneers List
- Index to Marriage Banns, 1900-1949
- Index to Miscellaneous Documents, 1859-1908
- Index to Organization and Church Papers, 1844-1919
- Index to Partnership Documents, 1846-1915
- Index to Probate Court Accounts & Inventories, Pre-1884
- Index to Probate Court Journals, 1858-1891
- Index to Recorder's Office Sundries, 1794-1889 (includes mortgages, leases, mechanics liens, etc.)
- Volume 1: Index of Recorded Court Records 1841-1869 (abbreviated index)
- Volume 2: index of Reported Court Records 1870-1879 (abbreviated index)
- Index to Veteran Discharges: Army 1859-1865, Navy 1859-1917
- Lease Index 1 (1858-1874)
- Marriage Index, 1808-1884 (abbreviated index)
- Recorder's Office Surname Deed indexes
- Index to Hamilton County, Ohio, Wills 1791-1850
- Archdiocese of Cincinnati Roman Catholic Baptism Records – Early-1859 (abbreviated indexes)

- Lineage Societies:
  - Index to First Families of Hamilton County, Ohio
  - Index to Settlers and Builders of Hamilton County, Ohio
  - Index to Century Families of Hamilton County, Ohio

Members-only databases
- Index to Church Deaths 1890-1899 (full index record)
- Index to Death Notices, 1827-1910 (full index record)
- Marriage Index, 1808-1884 (full index record)
- Master Index to Hamilton County Wills, 1918-1973 (on-going indexing project)
- Index to *Der Christliche Apologete* 1839-1899 (full index record)
- Weil Funeral Home – Funeral Records (OCR searchable PDF images)

Local records

Hamilton County records can be found in one location, multiple locations, and/or online. This section explains where to find local records. Each topic includes historical background, explanation of the types of records, how and when they were created, date ranges available, and tips on access and use.

- Births and Baptisms
- Cemeteries (includes several military burial databases)
- City and County Directories
- City and County Histories
- Court Records
- Death Notices and Obituaries
- Death Records (religious and civil records)
- Guardianships, Orphanages, Adoptions
- Land Records and Maps
- Recorder's Office Deed Indexes
- Marriages and Divorces
- Naturalizations
- Pioneers and Early Settlers
- Religious Records
- Wills, Probate and Estates

Hamilton County records repositories

This section covers the main repositories of physical and microfilm records of Hamilton County. Each topic includes the history and location of the repository, tips for visiting and locating records, and overviews of major collections held.

- Archives and Rare Books Library (University of Cincinnati)
- Cincinnati History Library and Archives (CHLA)
- Family History Centers (LDS)
- Public Library of Cincinnati and Hamilton County (PLCH)
- Hamilton County Probate Court
- Hamilton County Recorder's Office
- Religious Institutions

Research services

This web page describes the types of research offered by Hamilton County Genealogical Society, for a minimal fee, through the HCGS Research Committee. The page also includes a list of paid researchers who specialize in Hamilton County. These individuals operate independently of HCGS, and their contact information is included.

Surnames

The HCGS Surname Database includes the surnames of Hamilton County ancestors added by HCGS members since 2014. These are family names of interest to members. The public can search for surnames and contact the members via email to compare and share family ancestry.

Queries

After the creation of the Surname Database in 2014, HCGS stopped publishing queries in the *Tracer*. This section of the website includes the 2013 and 2014 queries and indexes of all surnames published in a genealogical context in the *Tracer* during 1981 through 1986, 1988 through 2005, and 2009 through 2013.

Publications

The *Gazette* (a quarterly newsletter) is available to the public. The online *Tracer* issues are available only to members. An index to *Tracer* article topics can be searched by the public. The indexes are broken down into the periods 1979-2008 and 2008-2018. Back issues of the *Tracer* are available for purchase on DVD or CD and available in hard copy at PLCH and major genealogical libraries.

Videos

HCGS posts videos of seminars and programs of interest to Hamilton County researchers. Many videos are accessible by the public.

Lineage societies

The names contained in the applications approved for the three Hamilton County lineage societies are indexed on the HCGS website. These names are also listed in finding aids on the website of the Cincinnati History Library and Archives (CHLA) which holds the application files.

Interest groups

Specific Interest Groups maintain separate pages in this section of the website. Currently the following interest groups are active. Their web pages contain resources including research tips, helpful publications and websites, videos, and programs.

- German Interest Group
- DNA Interest Group (Southwest Ohio DNA)
- Jewish Interest Group

Shop and support

HCGS has published many books that are available for purchase via the website. The publications are categorized for ease of browsing.

- Baptism Records
- Burial Records
- Death Records
- Funeral Home Records
- Marriage Records
- Other Publications
- Property Records, etc.

Hamilton County genealogy websites

This page provides categorized links for scanned records, transcriptions, databases, indexes, searchable lists, articles, books, maps, newspapers, images, histories, repository information, and finding aids, to enhance genealogical research in Hamilton County.

Digital Library

The Digital Library of the Public Library of Cincinnati and Hamilton County continues to digitize materials and provide them to the public at https://digital.cincinnatilibrary.org. This list includes the current collections and exhibits of particular interest to Hamilton County researchers. Some collections, such as Genealogy & Local History, include hundreds of items and are subdivided by topic.

For information about using the Digital Library, see these *Tracer* articles:

- "PLCH Digital Library: Free Access to Historic Hamilton County Resources," June 2015
- "The New Digital Library: Electronic Access to Thousands of Genealogy Materials," December 2015 (tips on searching and navigating)

Collections

19th Century Photography	Greater Cincinnati Memory Project
African-American Society Columns	History & Geography
Althea Hurst Scrapbook	Inland Rivers Library
Business, Shipping & Trade Directories	Inland Rivers Photograph Collection
Catholic Telegraph	Library History (PLCH)
Cincinnati Architecture	Local History Index
Cincinnati Better Housing League	Magazines & Newspapers
Cincinnati Businesses	Maps & Atlases
Cincinnati Camera Club	Nast-Trinity Methodist Church
Cincinnati Federation of Colored Women's Clubs	Ohio River Floods
Cincinnati History Lantern Slides	Oscar Wilde in Cincinnati
Cincinnati Panorama of 1848	Published in Cincinnati
Cincinnati Photo and Print File	Samuel Hannaford Architectural Drawings
Cincinnati Prints	Thomas Cottrell Collection of Bills of Lading and
Cincinnati Trade Catalogs	Freight Receipts
Cincinnati Vaudeville Programs	Veterans History Project
City & County Directories	World War I
Disabled American Veterans	World War I & II Propaganda Posters
Finding Aids & Inventories	Yearbooks
Genealogy & Local History	

Exhibits

Beneath the Banks: Investigating Cincinnati's Changing Riverfront
Bills of Lading - Viewing Cincinnati through Its River Trade
Cincinnati's Brewing and Drinking History
Cincinnati's Historic Architecture: An Overview of 150 Years of Architectural Styles
Green Acres [Cincinnati Horticulture]
Inventing an American Style: American Prints
Over Here and Over There
Queen City of Song
Revived Italian Architecture
Rivalries, Championships & Legends: 100 Years of Cincinnati High School Football
St. Bernard History
Streetcar History

FamilySearch Resources

FamilySearch has several digitized collections for the state of Ohio that include Hamilton County records as well as numerous items that can only be accessed through its catalog.

Ohio Collections with Hamilton County Records
https://www.familysearch.org/search > enter Ohio in Collection Title

Searchable (some collections may not be completely indexed):
- Ohio Births and Christenings, 1821-1962 (abstracts)
- Ohio Death Index, 1908-1932, 1938-1944, and 1958-2007 (abstracts)
- Ohio Deaths and Burials, 1854-1997 (abstracts)
- Ohio Deaths, 1908-1953 (images)
- Ohio Marriages, 1800-1958 (abstracts)
- Ohio, County Births, 1841-2003 (images)
- Ohio, County Death Records, 1840-2001 (images)
- Ohio, County Marriages, 1789-2013 (images)
- Ohio, County Naturalization Records, 1800-1977 (images)
- Ohio, Southern District Naturalization Index, 1852-1991 (images)
- Ohio, World War I Statement of Service Cards, 1914-1919 (abstracts)

Browseable images arranged by county and type:
- Ohio Probate Records, 1789-1996
- Ohio, Hamilton County Records, 1791-1994

Finding unindexed digitized images of microfilm

Only a fraction of the microfilms already digitized is in the Historical Collections on FamilySearch—and name searches will return results only for names already indexed, again a fraction of the available records. To find the rest of these records, search the FamilySearch catalog for specific places, subjects, and record types.

For example, none of Hamilton County's tax or church records are listed in Historical Collections, but the catalog contains a large number of local tax and church records digitized and available to view. Many unindexed digitized records will be found only by searching the catalog.

From the main screen at https://www.familysearch.org choose Search > Catalog > Search for: Place, Keyword, etc. Under Availability, click Online > Search. In the list of results, click on the title to see detailed information. Collections have the message "To view a digital version of this item, click here." For individual microfilms, click on the camera icon on the far right of the number to view the digital version. If the camera icon has a key, the film must be viewed in a Family History Center or a FamilySearch affiliate library (such as the Kenton County Public Library in Covington, Kentucky).

FamilySearch is digitizing a thousand microfilms each day, so check periodically to see if a film has been digitized.

To learn how to locate microfilm that has not yet been digitized, see "Going Through the Back Door to Find Microfilms," *The Tracer*, September 2018.

FamilySearch Catalog Subjects: Hamilton County, Ohio

https://www.familysearch.org/search/catalog > Hamilton County, Ohio

United States, Ohio, Hamilton	- Court records - Indexes (1)	- Maps - Indexes (1)
- Archives & libraries - Inventories, registers, catalogs (3)	- Directories (4)	- Military records (4)
- Archives and libraries - Sources (1)	- Genealogy (13)	- Military records - Revolution, 1775-1783 (2)
- Bible records (3)	- Genealogy - Handbooks, manuals, &c. (6)	- Minorities (1)
- Biography (6)	- Genealogy - Societies - Periodicals (1)	- Naturalization and citizenship (8)
- Biography - Indexes (2)	- Guardianship (5)	- Naturalization and citizenship - Indexes (2)
- Business records and commerce (1)	- Historical geography (1)	- Obituaries (1)
- Cemeteries (17)	- History (16)	- Probate records (19)
- Cemeteries - Indexes (1)	- History - Indexes (4)	- Probate records - Indexes (2)
- Cemeteries - Maps (1)	- History - Sources - Inventories, registers, catalogs (1)	- Public records (3)
- Census - 1870 (1)	- Land and property (14)	- Societies (2)
- Census - 1890 (1)	- Land and property - Indexes (1)	- Taxation (3)
- Census - Indexes - 1890 (1)	- Land and property - Inventories, registers, catalogs (1)	- Taxation - Indexes (1)
- Church history (1)	- Land and property - Maps (3)	- Vital records (29)
- Church records (7)	- Maps (5)	- Vital records - Indexes (4)
- Church records - Indexes (3)		- Voting registers (1)
- Court records (6)		

The number in parentheses after each topic is the number of items pertaining to the topic. Each item may consist of multiple rolls of microfilm, and some may be digitized.

FamilySearch Catalog Subjects: Cincinnati, Ohio

https://www.familysearch.org/search/catalog > Cincinnati, Ohio

United States, Ohio, Hamilton, Cincinnati	- Genealogy (9)- Genealogy - Archives and libraries - Directories (1)	- Minorities (7)
- Archives and libraries - Directories (1)	- Genealogy - Handbooks, manuals, etc. (5)	- Naturalization and citizenship (1)
- Archives and libraries -Inventories, registers, catalogs (5)	- Genealogy - Periodicals (2)	- Naturalization and citizenship - Indexes (2)
- Archives and libraries - Periodicals ( )	- Genealogy - Societies (1)	- Newspapers (17)
- Archives and libraries - Sources (1)	- History (37)	- Newspapers - Indexes (2)
- Bible records (1)	- History - Indexes (1)	- Obituaries (4)
- Bibliography (1)	- History - Periodicals (1)	- Obituaries - Indexes (10)
- Biography (16)	- History - Sources (2)	- Occupations - Directories (2)
- Biography - Indexes (1)	- Jewish records (3)	- Officials and employees - Biography (1)
- Biography - Portraits (1)	- Land and property (3)	- Periodicals (2)
- Cemeteries (37)	- Maps (10)	- Public records (3)
- Cemeteries - Indexes (1)	- Maps - Indexes (1)	- School yearbooks (22)
- Census - 1817 (1)	- Medical records (1)	- Schools (5)
- Census - 1870 (2)	- Military history - Civil War, 1861-1865 (2)	- Social life and customs (1)
- Census - 1920 - Maps (1)	- Military history - Civil War, 1861-1865 - Regimental histories (3)	- Societies (6)
- Centennial celebrations, etc. (1)	- Military records - Civil War, 1861-1865 (1)	- Vital records (13)
- Church history (46)	- Military records - Civil War, 1861-1865 Indexes (1)	- Vital records - Indexes (2)
- Church records (103)		- Vital records - Newspapers (2)
- Church records - Indexes (1)		- Vital records - Newspapers - Indexes (4)
- Directories (12)		
- Funeral homes (16)		

FamilySearch Wiki Topics: Hamilton County Genealogy

https://www.familysearch.org/wiki/en/Hamilton_County,_Ohio_Genealogy

1 Quick Dates	5 Resources	5.17 Periodicals
1.1 Boundary Changes	5.1 Getting Started	5.18 Probate Records
1.2 Record Loss	5.2 Research Guides	5.19 Taxation
2 Governmental Repositories	5.3 Bible Records.	5.20 Vital Records
2.1 County Courthouses	5.4 Cemeteries	5.20.1 Births
2.1.1 County Clerk of Courts	5.5 Census	5.20.2 Marriage
2.1.2 Probate Court	5.6 Church Records	5.20.3 Deaths
2.1.3 First District Court of	5.6.1 Court Records	5.21 Maps
Appeals	5.7 Directories	5.22 Repositories
2.2 Federal Courts in Hamilton	5.8 Ethnic, Political, or Religious	5.22.1 Family History
County	Groups	Centers
2.3 County Recorder and Auditor	5.9 Genealogy	5.22.2 Libraries
2.4 County Health Department	5.10 History	5.22.3 Societies
3 Historical Facts	5.11 Land and Property	5.22.3.1 Online
3.1 Description	5.12 Maps	Genealogy Research
3.2 Parent Jurisdictions	5.13 Migration	Groups
4 Places	5.14 Military	5.23 Websites
4.1 Populated Places	5.14.1 Civil War	5.24 Upcoming Events
4.2 Neighboring Counties	5.14.2 World War II	6 Sources Consulted
4.3 Family History Library	5.15 Naturalization and Citizenship	6.1 References
4.4 FamilySearch Wiki/Online	5.16 Newspapers	

FamilySearch Wiki Topics: Hamilton County Resources

https://www.familysearch.org/wiki/en/Hamilton_County,_Ohio_Resources

1 Resources online	6.8 U.S. Federal District Court 1803-present
2 Research Guides	6.9 U.S. Federal Circuit Courts 1807-1911
3 Cemeteries	7 Directories
3.1 Cemetery Deeds and Lot Owner Deeds	8 Ethnic, Political, or Religious Groups
3.2 Cemetery Records	8.1 African American
3.3 Cemetery Records Available Online	8.2 American Indian
4 Census	8.3 Germans
4.1 U.S. Population Census Schedules	9 Genealogy
4.2 U.S. Nonpopulation Census Schedules	10 History
4.3 State Census	11 Land and Property
5 Church Records	12 Maps
6 Court Records	13 Migration
6.1 Justice of the Peace - Township	14 Military
6.2 Northwest Territorial Court 1787-1803	14.1 Civil War
6.3 Court of Common Pleas/Cincinnati Municipal Court	15 Naturalization and Citizenship
6.4 Probate Court	16 Newspapers
6.5 Hamilton Co. District Court 1851-1883	17 Periodicals
6.6 Hamilton Co. Circuit Court 1883-1912	18 Probate Records
6.7 Ohio Supreme Court 1803-present	19 Taxation
	20 Vital Records

Other Genealogical Websites

See the HCGS web page, Hamilton County Genealogy Websites, https://hcgsohio.org/links.php?sid=1, for an additional list of websites with Hamilton County content.

Cemeteries and burial sites	
Billion Graves	https://billiongraves.com
Cincinnati Catholic Cemetery Society	https://cccsohio.org
Find a Grave	https://www.findagrave.com
Interment – Online Cemetery Records	http://www.interment.net/Default.htm
Jewish Cemeteries of Greater Cincinnati	https://www.jcemcin.org
Union Township Cemetery (Mt. Moriah)	www.union-township.oh.us/cemdb/index.aspx
DNA sites (see HCGS website for information on the SWOHDNA interest group and additional links)	
DNAGedcom	https://dnagedcom.com
Gedmatch Genesis	https://genesis.gedmatch.com
The Genetic Genealogist	https://thegeneticgenealogist.com
General research sites	
FamilySearch	https://www.familysearch.org
Gen Exchange	www.genexchange.com
HeritageQuest Research Library	https://hqrl.com
Wiki Tree	https://www.wikitree.com
German heritage sites	
Archion – German Evangelical Church Records	https://www.archion.de/en/the-portal
German-American Citizens' League	www.gacl.org
German Genealogical Word List	www.familysearch.org/wiki/en/German_Genealogical_Word_List
Germans in Hamilton County, Ohio	https://www.familysearch.org/wiki/en/Germans_in_Hamilton_County,_Ohio
Matricula – German Catholic Records Archives	https://data.matricula-online.eu/en
Meyers Gazetteer of the German Empire	https://www.meyersgaz.org
Hamilton County sites	
Cincinnati Catholic Genealogy	https://www.rootsweb.com/~ohhamilt/catholic/catholic.html
Hamilton County Auditor's Office	https://hamiltoncountyauditor.org
Hamilton County GenWeb	https://www.rootsweb.com/~ohhamilt/mnpg.html
Hamilton County Probate Court	www.probatect.org
Hamilton County Recorder's Office	https://recordersoffice.hamilton-co.org
Historical sites	
Cincinnati Preservation Association	www.cincinnatipreservation.org
Gorman Farm	www.gormanfarm.org
Sharon Woods Village	www.heritagevillagecincinnati.org
Land records, maps, and gazetteers	
Atlas of Historical County Boundaries - Ohio	https://publications.newberry.org/ahcbp/pages/Ohio.html

David Rumsey Map Collection	https://www.davidrumsey.com
Federal Land Patents (BLM)	https://glorecords.blm.gov
Historic Map Works – Residential Genealogy	www.historicmapworks.com
Map of US (interactive boundary changes)	https://www.mapofus.org/ohio

Libraries and archives

Allen County (IN) Public Library	www.acpl.lib.in.us
American Jewish Archives	http://americanjewisharchives.org
Archives and Rare Books Library, UC	www.libraries.uc.edu/libraries.arb
Archives of the Archdiocese of Cincinnati	www.catholiccincinnati.org/ministries-offices/archives-office
Cincinnati History Library and Archives	library.cincymuseum.org
Columbus Metropolitan Library	https://www.columbuslibrary.org
Midwest Genealogy Center	https://www.mymcpl.org/genealogy
Library of Congress	https://loc.gov
National Archives Resources for Genealogists	https://www.archives.gov/research/genealogy
Ohio History Connection (formerly Ohio Historical Society)	https://www.ohiohistory.org
Public Library of Cincinnati and Hamilton Co. Genealogy and Local History Department	https://www.cincinnatilibrary.org www.cincinnatilibrary.org/main/genlocal.html
Rutherford B. Hayes Presidential Center	http://www.rbhayes.org
University of Cincinnati Libraries Digital Resource Commons	https://drc.libraries.uc.edu

Miscellaneous sites

Behind the Name (first names)	www.behindthename.com
Castle Garden & New York (1830-1912)	http://castlegarden.org
Chronicling America	https://chroniclingamerica.loc.gov
Cincinnati Fire Department	www.cfdhistory.com
Cincinnati Police Historical Society Museum	http://police-museum.org
Cyndi's List of Genealogical Sites	https://www.cyndislist.com
Ellis Island Foundation	https://libertyellisfoundation.org
Google Books	https://books.google.com
Google Language Translator	https://translate.google.com
Latin Genealogical Word List	https://www-a1.familysearch.org/wiki/en/Latin_Genealogical_Word_List
LDS Genealogy - Cincinnati Genealogy	https://ldsgenealogy.com/OH/Cincinnati.htm
Linkpendium	http://www.linkpendium.com/hamilton-oh-genealogy
Miami Valley Ohio Genealogical Index	http://gen2.pcdl.lib.oh.us/miami/miami.htm
Morgan Library of Ohio Imprints, 1796-1850	http://morgan.mwa.org/ohionames
Ohio GenWeb	https://www.ohgenweb.org
Over-the-Rhine Chamber of Commerce	www.otrchamber.com
St. Joseph Orphanage	https://stjosephorphanage.org

Vital records

Ohio Death Certificate Index (1913-1944, 1954-1963)	https://resources.ohiohistory.org/death/#scroll
Ohio Department of Health	https://odh.ohio.gov

Chapter 8: Jurisdictions and Maps

Development of Townships

In 1853 Hamilton County had sixteen townships, but four no longer exist. Fulton, Mill Creek, Spencer, and Storrs were absorbed by Cincinnati and other towns as they grew and annexed nearby villages. Another township, South Bend, lasted only fourteen years before being split into two new townships. This list provides the beginning and ending dates of Hamilton County's townships, as reported by Marjorie Burress in *Early Rosters of Hamilton County* (based on Henry and Kate Ford's *History of Hamilton County, Ohio*, 1881, pages 69-70). These township names remain in use in the land records of Hamilton County.

TOWNSHIP	ESTABLISHED	HISTORY
Anderson	1793	Only township in Virginia Military District
Cincinnati	1791	Now City of Cincinnati
Colerain	1794	Originally included much of Butler County
Columbia	1791	One of the three original townships, with Cincinnati and Miami
Crosby	1804	Created from Whitewater
Delhi	1816	Created from Green
Fulton	1820-1826	Annexed to Cincinnati 1854
Green	1809	Created from South Bend
Harrison	1853	Created from Crosby and Whitewater
Miami	1791	
Mill Creek	1809	Created from Cincinnati Township, annexed to Cincinnati after 1930
South Bend	1795	Absorbed by Green and Delhi about 1809
Spencer	1830s	Created from Columbia, annexed to Cincinnati after 1880
Springfield	1797	
Storrs	1820s	Created from Delhi, annexed to Cincinnati about 1869
Sycamore	Ca 1800 or 1803	
Symmes	1820-1826	Created from Sycamore
Whitewater	1803	

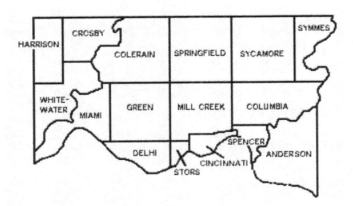

Outline map of 1869 townships, from http://www.emslanders.com/HamiltonCoOH.htm#HamiltonOHTwps, based on a map in the David Rumsey Historical Map Collection, https://www.davidrumsey.com

Current Townships and Municipalities

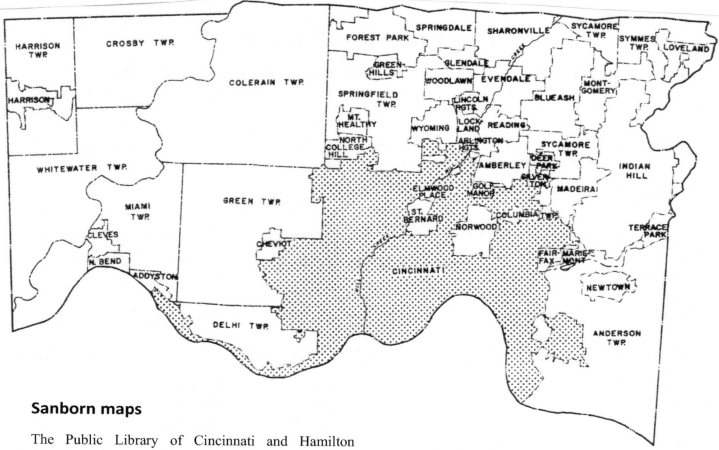

Sanborn maps

The Public Library of Cincinnati and Hamilton County's Digital Library has full color Sanborn Fire Insurance Maps (in the Maps and Atlases section). These large-scale street plans of various years between 1887 and 1937 show building outlines, property boundaries, and building use.

Tracer articles about maps

See the February 2009 issue of *The Tracer* for five articles about using Sanborn maps at PLCH and CHLA. Other map articles:

- "Hamilton County Maps, 1835-2017," March 2018
- "Cincinnati Maps, 1792-2017," June 2018
- "Digital Maps and Atlases at the Public Library of Cincinnati and Hamilton County," June 2018
- "Cincinnati and Hamilton County Map Research at PLCH," June 2018

Dates of Annexation of Cincinnati Suburbs, 1802-1982

When looking for vital records of people who lived in the Cincinnati area, it is important to know whether the place where they lived was within the city limits at the time of the event. This map giving dates of annexation for various parts of the city is from page 116 of *Cincinnati Then and Now* by Iola Silberstein and is reproduced with the permission of the author.

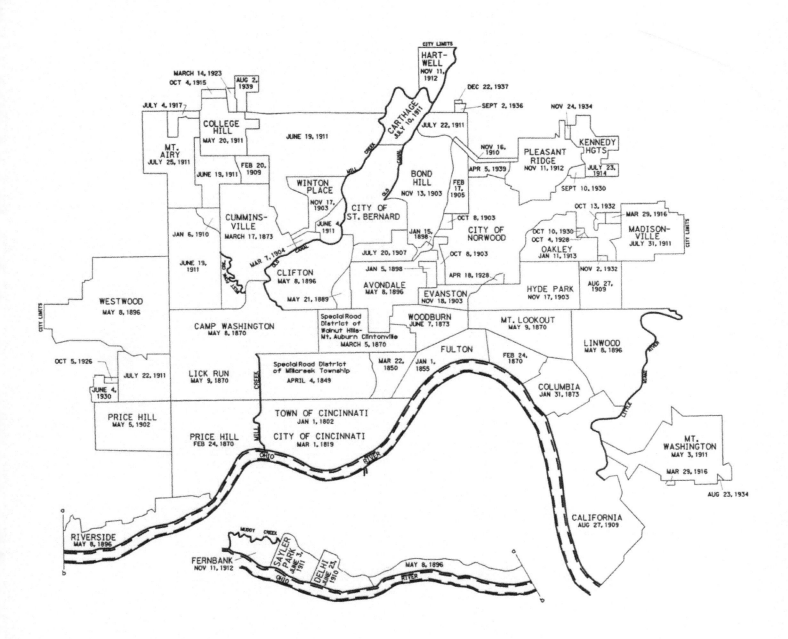

Discontinued Post Offices

These post offices are not mentioned in the Gazetteer starting on page 98. See *The Post Offices of Ohio* by John S. Gallagher and Alan H. Patera, published in 1979, for a complete list of post offices and more details of interest.

POST OFFICE	ESTABLISHED	DISCONTINUED	RELOCATED IN
Beechwood	1884	1888	Delhi
Bevis Tavern	1835	1838	Bevis
Biddinger	1900	1900	Harrison
Brough	1882	1887	Blue Ash
Browns Grove	1843	1852	Mt. Airy
Carey's Academy	1842	1849	College Hill
Carson's Tavern	1818	1825	Cheviot
Challensville	1843	1846	Dent
Charleston			See Round Bottom Mills
Clarks Store	1827	1842	Not Listed
Cologne	1887	1888	Mt. Healthy
Columbia Park	1927	1957	North Bend
Dry Fork	1851	1853	Not Listed
East Sycamore	1858	1884	Carthage
Fort Scott Camps	1941	1976	Harrison
Fosdick	1852	1854	Glendale
Grand Valley	1870	1882	Camp Dennison
Hutchisons	1828	1829	Not Listed
Hygeia	1850	1852	Not Listed
Karr	1880	1888	Harrison
Lilac	1894	1898	Harrison
McWhorter	1876	1878	Evendale
Mears Farm	1830	1846	Mt. Washington
Mechanics Row	1833	1835	Not Listed
Medoc	1863	1864	Not Listed
Milldale	1885	1890	Rossmoyne
Millersville	1807	1816	Not Listed
Moselle	1881	1883	Silverton
Ourys	1830	1856	Not Listed
Pleasant Hill	1837	1842	Careys Academy
Preston	1825	1903	Harrison
Red Bank	1886	1905	Linwood
Revere	1892	1895	Miami
Round Bottom Mills	1804	1816	Not Listed
Snyder	1891	1904	Cincinnati
South Pendleton	1859	1874	Not Listed
Springfield	1813	1828	Springdale
Storrs	1851	1871	Not Listed
Tompkins	1852	1865	California

Renumbering of Cincinnati Buildings

Official house numbers were first assigned in 1853. Until then, all directory "addresses" were imprecise. Starting in 1853 the house numbers indicated the side of the street: even on east and north, odd on west and south (this rule has never changed). Then in 1896 (1895 for businesses), all house numbers in Cincinnati were changed based on an improved system. Numbers on all streets jumped to a new hundred at each block, and Vine Street became the dividing line for distinguishing streets as east or west. Until 1895, Main Street had been the dividing line.

Street Name Changes

In 1802 there were two competing lists of names for Cincinnati streets, one submitted by Israel Ludlow and one by Joel Williams. Israel Ludlow's list prevailed. Some early Hamilton County deeds or other records may refer to the street name used by Williams. The differences in these two lists are noted below.

Israel Ludlow list	Joel Williams list	Early street name changes
Third Street	Hill Street	Western Row renamed Central Avenue
Fourth Street	High Street	Eastern Row renamed Broadway
Fifth Street	Byrd Street	Catherine Street renamed Court Street (part)
Sixth Street	Gano Street	Abigail Street renamed 12th Street
Seventh Street	Northern Row	
Walnut Street	Cider Street	
Vine Street	Jefferson Street	
Race Street	Beech Street	
Plum Street	Filson Street	

During the anti-German hysteria of World War I, twelve street names were changed in Cincinnati:

Berlin Street renamed Woodrow Street
Bremen Street renamed Republic Street
Brunswick Place renamed Edgecliff Point
German Street renamed English Street
Frankfort Avenue renamed Connecticut Avenue
Hamburg Street renamed Stonewall Street

Hanover Street renamed Yukon Street
Hapsburg Street renamed Merrimac Street
Humboldt Avenue renamed William Howard Taft Road
Schumann Street renamed Beredith Place
Vienna Street renamed Panama Street
Wilhelm Street renamed Orion Street

Additional street name changes

(Old) 2nd Street renamed Pete Rose Way in 1985
Amity Road (in Deer Park) renamed Galbraith Road
Armory Ave. renamed Derrick Turnbow Ave. in 1991
Columbia Ave. renamed Columbia Parkway ca. 1936
Eastern Avenue (part) changed to Riverside Dr., 2009

Lincoln Park Drive renamed Ezzard Charles
Lodge Alley renamed Ruth Lyons Alley
Martin Place renamed Adams Crossing in 1990
Produce Drive renamed Theodore M. Berry Way, 1997
Van Zandt (North College Hill) renamed Galbraith Rd.

Dixmyth/St. Clair/Melish (part) renamed Martin Luther King Drive in 1987
N. & S. Crescent Avenues renamed Fred Shuttlesworth Circle in 1998

Street name changes circa 1910 – 1930s catalogued by Steve Morse:
https://www.stevemorse.org/census/changes/CincinnatiChanges.htm

To inquire about street name changes in the City of Cincinnati, contact the Department of Transportation & Engineering, Engineering Division/Right of Way Management, at (513) 352-2366. For Hamilton County street name changes, contact the Hamilton County Engineer's Office, which has road records, at (513) 946-4250.

Gazetteer of Hamilton County, Ohio, 1784–1986

This gazetteer is based on the 1911/12 Hamilton County directory, supplemented by Hamilton County directories in 1893, 1915, 1939, 1940, 1942, 1944, 1957, 1958, 1959, 1960, 1961, 1963 and 1964; *History of Hamilton County, Ohio* by Henry A. & Kate B. Ford, 1881; *Cincinnati, The Queen City, 1788–1912* by Rev. Charles F. Goss; *1869 Atlas of Cincinnati & Hamilton County, Ohio*, by C. O. Titus; *Place Names Directory of Southwest Ohio* (1986) by Madge R. Fitak; 2000 Hamilton County map.

Addyston - Miami Township - west of Cincinnati on Ohio River (US 50) - pop. 500 in 1911 - Incorporated 1891

Allandale - Symmes Township - P.O. Loveland & Madisonville in 1911 - SW corner of township

Amberley Village - Sycamore & Columbia Townships - added to Hamilton Co. Directory 1946 - established 1940

Anderson Ferry - Delhi Township - Anderson Ferry Rd. & US 50

Anderson Station - see Anderson Ferry - on 1880 map

Anderson Township - established 1793

Arlington Heights - Springfield & Sycamore Townships -P.O. Lockland in 1911 - pop. 500 in 1911

Asbury - Anderson Township - one mile south of Forestville - P.O. California in 1911

Avoca Park - Columbia Twp. - P.O. Madisonville 1911

Avondale - Mill Creek Township - annexed to Cincinnati in 1896 - on Reading Rd. - established 1854

Barnesburg - Colerain Township - on Blue Rock Pike - P.O. Mt. Healthy in 1911

Barnsburg - Colerain Township - alternate spelling of Barnesburg

Barrsville - Mill Creek Township – annexed to Cincinnati in 1870

Batavia Junction - Columbia Township

Beechwood - Symmes Township - P.O. Rossmoyne 1911

Berea - Whitewater Township - established 1817 - "mostly a town on paper" as it did not develop

Bevis - Colerain Township - on Colerain Pike - P.O. Mt. Healthy in 1911- established 1820s

Big Bottom - Symmes Township

Blue Ash - Sycamore Township - added to Hamilton County Directory in 1946 - Incorporated 1955

Blue Jay - added to Hamilton County Directory in 1939 - Whitewater Township - near Harrison Ave. & Strimple Rd.

Bond Hill - Mill Creek Township - annexed to Cincinnati in 1903 - established 1870

Braggs Subdivision - annexed to Cincinnati in 1898

Brecon - Sycamore Township - on Kemper Rd. - P.O. Sharonville in 1911

Brentwood - Springfield Township - on Winton Rd. - a development within Finneytown

Bridgetown - Green Township - on Cleves Pike - west of Cheviot

Brighton - part of Cincinnati - east of Spring Grove Ave.

Broadwell - Anderson Township - at Mt. Carmel & Broadwell Rds.

Bucktown - area east of Broadway between 6th & 7th Sts. to Culvert St.

Cadbury - Whitewater Township - established 1802

California - Anderson Township - east of Cincinnati (US 52) - established 1849 - annexed to Cincinnati in 1909

Camden City - Columbia Township - on US 50 (Wooster Pike) - established 1857 - on 1880 map

Camp Dennison - Symmes Township - permanent village after 1866 - Civil War camp - Incorporated 1872

Camp Washington - Mill Creek Township - annexed to Cincinnati in 1870 - Hopple St. & Colerain Ave.

Campbell's Station - Colerain Township - 7 or 8 miles SE of Dunlap Station - established 1793

Carthage - Mill Creek & Springfield Townships - on Vine Street - pop. 4000 in 1911 - established 1815 - annexed to Cincinnati in 1911

Cedar Grove - Green Township (1893 Directory states it is in Delhi Township)

Cedar Point - Anderson Township - changed to Ellenora - formerly called Taylor's Corner - established 1845

Centretown - Springfield Twp.

Cherry Grove - Anderson Township - on Ohio Pike (Beechmont Ave.)

Chester Park - Mill Creek Township - on Spring Grove Ave. - P.O. Winton Place 1911 - pop. 400 in 1911

Cheviot – previously in Green Township - on Harrison Pike - pop. 2400 in 1911 - established 1818

Cincinnati - Cincinnati Township - original settlement in 1788 - originally called Losantiville - county seat of Hamilton County

Cincinnati Township - now part of Cincinnati - established 1791

Clare - Columbia Township - only in 1915 Hamilton Co. Directory

Cleves - Miami Township - established 1818 - formerly called Clevestown - Incorporated 1874

Clevestown - Miami Township - established 1818 - now called Cleves

Clifton - Mill Creek Township - annexed to Cincinnati in 1896 - established 1849

Clifton Heights - Mill Creek Township - 1870 part of Cincinnati - near Clifton

Clintonville - annexed to Cincinnati in 1870

Clough - Anderson Township - on Clough Pike - one mile east of Mt. Washington - P.O. Newtown

Cluff - Anderson Township - on Cluff Pike - one mile east of Mt. Washington - P.O. Newtown

Coal City - Miami Township - later called Sekitan - now part of Addyston

Colerain Township - established 1794

Colerain Village - Colerain Township - early name for Dunlap Station

College Hill - Mill Creek & Springfield Township on Hamilton Pike - pop 2300 in 1911 - Incorporated 1857 - annexed to Cincinnati in 1911

Columbia - originally in Columbia Township and later Spencer Township - east of Cincinnati on Ohio River - original settlement in 1788 - annexed to Cincinnati in 1872

Columbia Township - established in 1791

Compton Estates - added to Hamilton Co. Directory 1964

Coney Island - Anderson Township - east of California on US 52 - formerly Parker's Grove

Corryville - Mill Creek Township - 1870 part of Cincinnati

Covalt's Station - Anderson Township - on Round Bottom Rd. - established 1790

Covedale - Green Township - at Cleves -Warsaw and Anderson Ferry Rds. - added to Hamilton County Directory in 1939

Creedville - Colerain & Green Townships - on Blue Rock Pike

Crescentville - Sycamore Township - partly in Butler County, OH

Crestvue - Springfield Township - on Princeton Pike - P.O. Sharonville 1911

Crosby Township - Harrison Township formed out of part of Crosby Township in 1853

Crosby Village - Crosby Township - established 1803

Culloms - Delhi Township - also called West Riverside

Cumminsville - Mill Creek Township - annexed to Cincinnati in 1872 - on this site Ludlow Station was established in 1790

Deer Park - Sycamore Township - P.O. Silverton in 1911 - established 1886

Delhi - Delhi Township - established 1866 - Incorporated 1885 - annexed to Cincinnati in 1910

Delhi Township - established 1817 - portions annexed to Cincinnati in 1902 - formed from Green Township

Dent - Green Township - on Harrison Pike

Devins Station - Miami Township - on 1869 Atlas - on Ohio River

Dillonvale - Sycamore Township - at Galbraith & Plainfield Rds.

Dornbusch - Sycamore Township

Dry Ridge - Colerain Township - on Dry Ridge Rd.

Dry Ridge - Green Township - west of Bridgetown

Dunlap - Colerain Township - on Colerain Pike - formerly called Georgetown - P.O. Mt. Healthy in 1911

Dunlap Station - Colerain Township - established 1790 - also called Colerain Village

East Columbia - Spencer Township - now in Cincinnati

East End - eastern side of downtown Cincinnati – on Riverside Drive (formerly Eastern Ave.) & Columbia Ave. (now Parkway)

East Price Hill - Storrs Township - annexed to Cincinnati in 1870

East Norwood - Columbia Township

East Walnut Hills - 1870 part of Cincinnati

Edgemont - Springfield Township - near Carthage

Edgemont Terrace - added to Hamilton Co. Directory 1964

Eight Mile - Anderson Township - on Eight Mile Rd.

Elizabethtown - Whitewater Township - on the Whitewater & Big Miami Rivers - established 1817 (or as early as 1806?)

Ellenora - Anderson Township - formerly Cedar Point

Elliston - Springfield Township - established 1868

Elmwood Place - Mill Creek Township - on Vine Street - pop. 4200 in 1911 - established 1875

Elsmere - Columbia Township - only in 1893 Hamilton County Directory - part of Norwood

Euclid - Columbia Township - See Kennedy (Heights)

Evanston - annexed to Cincinnati in 1903

Evendale - Sycamore Township - on Reading Rd. - P.O. Sharonville in 1911 - Incorporated 1951

Fairfax - Columbia Township - added to Hamilton County Directory in 1939

Fairmount - Mill Creek Township - part of Cincinnati on the west side in 1870

Fairview - now part of Cincinnati near Clifton

Fernald - Crosby Township - 1½ miles from New Baltimore - P.O. Harrison in 1911

Fernbank - Delhi & Miami Townships (also spelled Fern Bank) - Incorporated 1888 - annexed to Cincinnati 1912 - 6 miles west of Sedamsville

Finneytown - Springfield Township - on Winton Rd. - added to Hamilton County Directory in 1959

Five Corners - Green Township

Five Mile - Anderson Township - on Five Mile Rd.

Forbusville - Mill Creek Township - on annexed to Cincinnati 1870

Forestville - Anderson Township - on Ohio Pike (Beechmont Ave.)

Forest Park - Springfield Township - on Winton Rd. - added to Hamilton County Directory in 1963

Fort Finney - by mouth of the Great Miami River - established 1785

Foster Hill - Springfield Township - south of Woodlawn - one of the first settlements in Springfield Township

Fruit Hill - Anderson Township - on Ohio Pike (Beechmont Ave.) - P.O. Mt. Washington 1911

Fulton - Fulton Township - on Riverside Drive (formerly Eastern Ave.) - annexed to Cincinnati 1854

Fulton Township - now part of Cincinnati - east side - existed 1820s to 1854

Georgetown - Colerain Township - now called Dunlap

Gerard's Station - Anderson Township - established 1790

Germany - Symmes Township - established 1840 - south of Camp Dennison

Gilead - Delhi Township

Glendale - Springfield Township - on Sharon Rd. - pop. 2400 in 1911 - Incorporated 1855 or 1871

Glenwood - Symmes Township - NE of Allandale

Golf Manor - Columbia Township - added to Hamilton County Directory in 1944 - Incorporated in 1947

Gravel Pit - Miami Township

Gravelotte - Columbia Township - one mile SW of Camden City - established 1873

Green Township - established from South Bend Township - established in 1809

Greenhills - Springfield Township - on Winton Rd. - established 1938

Greenwood - Springfield Township - established 1858 - between Lockland & Wyoming

Griffin's Station - Springfield Township - established about 1793

Griffiths - Miami Township

Groesbeck - Colerain Township - on Colerain Pike - P.O. Mt. Healthy in 1911

Hamilton County - established in 1790 - Original County

Hamiltown - Mill Creek Township - on 1869 atlas

Harrison - Harrison Township - on Whitewater River - on Harrison Pike - established 1813

Harrison Township - established 1853 from Crosby & Whitewater Townships

Hartwell - Springfield Township - on Vine Street - P.O. Lockland in 1911- pop. 2500 in 1911 - established 1868 - Incorporated 1876 - annexed to Cincinnati in 1912

Hazelwood - Sycamore Township - NE of Blue Ash

Henry Runyan's Station - Sycamore Township - 1½ miles north of Reading - established in 1700s

High Point – north edge of Sycamore Township

Highland Grove – now part of Blue Ash

Hill & Dale - added to Hamilton County Directory 1964

Home City - Delhi Township - now Sayler Park - established 1849 - Incorporated 1879

Hooven - Whitewater Township - one mile west of Cleves - P.O. Cleves in 1911 - formerly known as Berea

Hopewell - Symmes Township - 4 miles NE of Montgomery

Hunt's Grove - Whitewater Township - only in 1893 Hamilton County Directory

Hyde Park - Columbia Township - annexed to Cincinnati in 1903 - earlier called Mornington

Indian Hill - Columbia Township - Incorporated 1941

Indian View - Columbia Township

Industry - Delhi Township - established 1847

Irvina - Green Twp.

Ivanhoe - Mill Creek Township - only in 1893 Hamilton County Directory

Ivorydale - Mill Creek Township - near St. Bernard

Kennedy (Heights) - Columbia Township - pop. 700 in 1911 - annexed to Cincinnati in 1914

Kenwood - Sycamore Township - added to Hamilton County Directory in 1944

Keys' Hill - Mill Creek Township - early name for Mt. Auburn until 1837

Lester - Columbia Township

Lewiston - Spencer Township - established 1828

Lick Run - Mill Creek Township - annexed to Cincinnati in 1869 - west side

Lincoln Heights - Springfield Township - added to Hamilton County Directory in 1957 – formerly part of Woodlawn

Linwood - Spencer Township - annexed to Cincinnati in 1896 - established 1848

Linwood Station - on 1869 Atlas & 1880 map - south of Linwood

Little Buck - vicinity of 6th & Freeman

Lockland - Springfield & Sycamore Townships - on the Miami Canal - pop. 4000 in 1911 - established 1829 - Incorporated 1865 - city in 1930

Long Wood - Mill Creek Township - on Winton Rd. - on 1869 Atlas

Losantiville - original name of Cincinnati

Loveland - in Warren, Clermont & Hamilton Counties - on the Little Miami River - pop. 2000 in 1911 - established 1848

Lower Price Hill - now part of Cincinnati on the west side

Ludlow Grove - Mill Creek Township - now incorporated within St. Bernard

Ludlow Station - Mill Creek Township - established 1790 - later changed to Cumminsville

McCullough's - Columbia Township

Mack - Green Township - on Cleves Pike

Madeira - Columbia & Sycamore Townships - pop. 400 in 1911 - established 1871

Madison - Columbia Township - now called Madisonville - established 1809

Madison Place - Columbia Township - added to Hamilton County Directory in 1939

Madisonville - Columbia Township - formerly called Madison - pop. 5600 in 1911 - established 1829 - Incorporated 1836 - annexed to Cincinnati 1911

Maplewood - Springfield Township - north of Hartwell - P.O. Lockland in 1911 - established 1873

Mariemont - Columbia Township - added to Hamilton County Directory in 1939 - established 1922 - Incorporated 1941

McFarland Station - Columbia Township - now called Pleasant Ridge

Mercer's Station - Anderson Township - now called Newtown - established 1792 - see Mercersburgh

Mercersburgh - Anderson Township - now called Newtown - established 1792

Miami - Whitewater Township - on the Big Miami River - on Harrison Pike - P.O. Cleves in 1911

Miami Township - established 1791

Miamitown - Whitewater Township - on the Great Miami River - on Harrison Pike - P.O. Cleves in 1911 - established 1816

Milford - in Clermont & Hamilton Counties - on the Little Miami River

Mill Creek Township - established 1809 - part annexed to Cincinnati in 1904 - existed until after 1930

Millvale - west of the Mill Creek between North Fairmount and Cumminsville

Mineola - Delhi Township - near Riverside - established 1873

Mohawk - part of Cincinnati - at Mohawk & McMicken Aves.

Monfort Heights - Green Township - at North Bend and West Fork Rds. - added to Hamilton County Directory in 1939

Montauk - Columbia Township - ½ mile NW of Camden City - near Clermont County line

Monterey – Delhi Township – established 1893

Montgomery - Sycamore Township - on Montgomery Pike - established 1794 - village founded 1805

Montgomery Station - Symmes Township - on 1869 Atlas

Mornington - Columbia Township - only in 1893 Hamilton County Directory - early name for Hyde Park

Morrisania - Springfield Township - on 1880 map

Moscow - Delhi Township - extinct by 1881

Mt. Adams - Cincinnati Township - part of Cincinnati – formerly Mt. Ida.

Mt. Airy - Mill Creek & Green Townships - Incorporated 1865 - annexed to Cincinnati in 1911

Mt. Auburn - Mill Creek Township - annexed to Cincinnati in 1870

Mt. Harrison - Mill Creek Township – annexed to Cincinnati 1870

Mt. Healthy - Springfield Township - on Hamilton Pike - formerly Mt. Pleasant - established 1817

Mt. Ida – changed name to Mt. Adams.

Mt. Lookout - Columbia Township - Incorporated in 1871- 1870 part of Cincinnati

Mt. Peter - Delhi Township - on Delhi Pike

Mt. Pleasant - Springfield Township - on Hamilton Pike – change name to Mt. Healthy in 1850 - established 1817

Mt. St. Joseph - Delhi Township - P.O. St. Joseph's Mother House in 1911

Mt. Summit - Anderson Township - on Clough Pike

Mt. Tusculum - Spencer Township - also called Tusculum - now part of Cincinnati

Mt. Washington - Anderson Township - established 1838 - Incorporated 1867 - annexed to Cincinnati 1911

Nelson's Station - Columbia Township - fort near Madisonville, mentioned in early histories

New Baltimore - Crosby Township - on Big Miami River - on Blue Rock & Baltimore Pike - established 1819

New Burlington - Springfield Township - on Hamilton Pike - two miles north of Mt. Healthy - established 1816

New Haven - Crosby Township - on Harrison Pike - 5 miles from Harrison - established 1815

Newtown - Anderson Township - on Batavia Pike (RT 32)

North Avondale - Mill Creek Township - now part of Cincinnati - on Reading Rd.

North Bend - Miami Township - off US 50 - original settlement 1789 - Incorporated 1874

North College Hill - Springfield Township - between College Hill and Mt. Healthy - village in 1916 - city in 1941

Northbrook - added to Hamilton County Directory 1964

Northern Liberties - area north of Northern Row (now Liberty Street) - 1st suburb annexed to Cincinnati

Northside - now part of Cincinnati – near Cumminsville

Norwood - Columbia & Mill Creek Townships - on Montgomery Pike - formerly Sharpsburgh - Incorporated 1888 - city in 1902

Oakley - Columbia Township - on Madisonville Pike (now Madison Rd.) - established 1870 - nicknamed Shusterville - annexed to Cincinnati 1913

Oak Hills - Unincorporated area of Green Township near Ebenezer Rd.

O'Bryanville/O'Bryonville/O'Bryonsville - Spencer Township - on Madison Rd. - established 1875 - now part of Cincinnati

Oklahoma - Mill Creek Township - annexed to Cincinnati in 1904

Over-the-Rhine - Cincinnati Township - part of Cincinnati - north and east of Central Parkway

Paddock Hills - Mill Creek Township - north of North Avondale

Park Place - Springfield Township - (near Wyoming) - P.O. Lockland in 1911 - established 1877

Parker's Grove - Anderson Township - now called Coney Island

Parkview Heights – Springfield Township - off North Bend Rd. east of Winton Rd.

Peach Grove - Colerain Township - on Springdale Rd.

Pendleton - Spencer Township – annexed to Cincinnati 1870

Petersborough - Delhi Township - two miles from Warsaw

Plainville - Columbia Township - on US 50 (Wooster Pike) - Established 1853

Pleasant Ridge - Columbia Township - on Montgomery Pike - annexed to Cincinnati in 1912 - established 1832

Pleasant Run - Springfield & Colerain Townships & Hamilton, OH - P.O. Mt. Healthy in 1911

Pleasant Valley - Anderson Township - in 1881 Hamilton County History

Polktown - Symmes Township - established 1817 - later called Symmes Station

Porkopolis - nickname of Cincinnati due to the hog and cattle slaughtering industry

Preston - Columbia Township - only in 1893 Hamilton County Directory

Price Hill - Storrs Township - annexed to Cincinnati in 1870 - west side

Queen City of the West - name bestowed on Cincinnati by Henry Wadsworth Longfellow during a visit

Queensgate - part of downtown Cincinnati - west of Central Ave.

Ramona - Columbia Township - P.O. Madisonville 1911

Rapid Run - Delhi Township

Red Bank Station - Spencer Township - later Columbia Township - on 1880 map

Reading - Sycamore Township - established 1795 (or 1804) - Incorporated 1851 - city 1930 - earlier called Vorheestown

Remington – Symmes Township - P.O. Blue Ash, Madisonville & Loveland in 1911 - on SR 126

Rensselaer Park - Springfield Township - west of Hartwell - P.O. Lockland in 1911

Ridgewood Acres - added to Hamilton County Directory in 1964

Rittner Station - Whitewater Township - on 1880 map

Riverdale - Whitewater Township - on 1869 Atlas - near Elizabethtown

Riverside - annexed to Cincinnati 1896 - on US 50, west side of Cincinnati - established as early as 1800 - Incorporated 1867

Rolling Ridge - Mill Creek Township - one mile north of Winton Place - on old Winton Rd.

Rose Hill - annexed to Cincinnati in 1898

Roselawn - now part of Cincinnati - on Reading Rd.

Rossmoyne - Sycamore Township - north of Deer Park

Ruffner Station - Whitewater Township - on 1869 Atlas

Runyan's Station - see Henry Runyan's Station

Russell's - Spencer Township - between Columbia & Red Bank

St. Bernard - Mill Creek Township - established 1850 - Incorporated 1878 - city 1912

St. Jacobs - Green Township - on 1869 Atlas & 1880 map

St. Peter's-Lick Run/St. Peterstown - Mill Creek Township - on 1869 Atlas - see St. Peter's - Lick Run

Sater - Crosby Township - only in 1893 Hamilton County Directory

Sayler Park - Delhi Township - on US 50 (River Rd.) formerly Home City - established 1849 - Incorporated 1879 - annexed to Cincinnati in 1911

Sedamsville - Delhi Township - on US 50 (River Rd.) - west side - Incorporated 1835 - annexed to Cincinnati 1870

Sekitan - Miami Township - formerly Coal City - west of Addyston

Shademoore - Anderson or Columbia Township - P.O. Plainville in 1911

Shaker Society - see Whitewater Village - established 1820s

Sharon - Sycamore Township - early name for Sharonville

Sharpsburg - Columbia Township - now called Norwood - established 1868

Sheartown - Green Township - on Harrison Pike - NW corner of township

Shorts Station - Miami Township - on US 50 - on 1869 Atlas & on 1880 map

Shrewsbury - possibly located in what is now Whitewater Township - established 1803

Shusterville - Columbia Township - early nickname for Oakley

Silverton - Columbia & Sycamore on Montgomery Pike - Incorporated 1904

Simonson's Station - Harrison Township - only in 1893 Hamilton County Directory

Sixteen-Mile Stand - Symmes Township - on Montgomery Pike - 4 miles north of Montgomery

Skyline Acres - added to Hamilton County Directory 1964 - mostly in Colerain Twp. on Springfield Twp. line

South Bend - Delhi Township - a short-lived community established about 1789 - later called Trautman

South Bend Township - original name of what closely resembled Delhi & Green Townships

Southside - Delhi Township - between Riverside & Mineola

Spencer Township - established 1830s to after 1880 - most annexed to Cincinnati in 1869

Spring Garden - Mill Creek Township - annexed to Cincinnati 1870

Springfield Township - established 1795

Springdale - Springfield Township - on Springfield Pike (RT 4) - established 1806 - Incorporated 1839 - city 1959

Steele Subdivision - Springfield Township - now called West College Hill

Storrs Township - annexed to Cincinnati in 1869 - west of the Mill Creek - existed 1820s to 1869

Sugar Camp Settlement - Miami Township - two miles from the Indiana line

Sweetwine/Sweet Wine - Anderson Township - on US 52

Sycamore Church - Symmes Township - 1880 map - on Montgomery Rd. - four miles NE of Montgomery

Sycamore Township - established 1803 - Symmes Township formed from eastern part of Sycamore Township between 1820 & 1826

Symmes Purchase - established 1787 - north of the Ohio River between the Great & Little Miami Rivers

Symmes (Station) - Symmes Township - earlier called Polktown - established 1817

Symmes Township - established between 1820 & 1826 - formed from eastern part of Sycamore Township

Taylor's Corner - Anderson Township - see Cedar Point - established 1845

Taylor's Creek/Taylor Creek - Colerain Township - on Harrison Pike at Springdale Rd.

Terra Alta - Sycamore Township - P.O. Blue Ash 1911

Terrace Park - Columbia Township - on US 50 (Wooster Pike) - established 1791 - Incorporated 1893

Texas - downtown area of old Cincinnati, northwest

Tower Hill - Columbia Township

Transit - Springfield Township - only in 1893 Hamilton County Directory

Trautman's Station - Delhi Township - on 1880 map - earlier called South Bend

Turkey Bottom - Spencer Township - between the Little Miami River & Columbia

Tusculum - Spencer Township - 1872 part of Cincinnati (on US 50) - also called Mt. Tusculum

Twightwee - Symmes Township

Undercliff - Spencer Township - between Columbia & Red Bank – 1872 part of Cincinnati

University Heights - now part of Cincinnati - near Clifton

Valley Junction - Whitewater Township - P.O. Cleves 1911 - only a station house with 2 or 3 dwellings

Virginia Military District - all of Anderson Township from 1784 to 1790

Vorhees Station - see Vorheestown

Vorheestown - Sycamore Township - early name for Reading - established 1795 or 1804

Walnut Hills - Mill Creek Township - annexed to Cincinnati in 1850 & 1870

Warsaw - Delhi Township - on 1869 Atlas & on 1880 map - NE corner of township

Weaversburg - Mill Creek Township - on 1869 Atlas

Weisenburgh/Wisenburg - Green Township
West College Hill - Springfield Township - formerly called Steele Subdivision
West End - the west end of downtown Cincinnati
West Fairmount - Mill Creek Township - on 1869 Atlas
West Price Hill - now part of Cincinnati
West Milford - Columbia Township - a part of Milford that is in Hamilton County
West Riverside - Delhi Township - also called Culloms
Westwood - Green Township - Harrison & Montana Aves. Incorporated 1868 - annexed to Cincinnati in 1896
Western Hills - the area west of the Cincinnati suburbs
White Oak - Colerain Township - on Cheviot & Blue Rock Rds. - added to Hamilton County Directory 1939
White's Station - Springfield Township - established about 1790
Whitewater Park - Whitewater Township
Whitewater Village - Crosby Township - Shaker settlement - one mile north of New Haven - established 1820s - on 1880 map as Shaker Society
Whitewater Township - established 1803 - Harrison Township formed out of part of Whitewater Township in 1853
Williamsdale - Springfield Township - now Rensselaer Park
Winslow Park - Sycamore Township - P.O. Sharonville in 1911 - between Hazelwood & Blue Ash
Winton Hills - Mill Creek Township
Winton Place - Mill Creek Township - annexed to Cincinnati in 1903 - established 1865
Winton Terrace - Mill Creek Township - north of Winton Place
Wintondale - Springfield Township - housing development in Finneytown - near Winton & Galbraith Rds.
Wisenburg/Weisenburgh - Green Township - on 1880 map
Woodburn - Mill Creek Township - annexed to Cincinnati 1872
Wooden Shoe Hollow - Mill Creek Township - north of Winton Place - on old Winton Rd.
Woodlawn - Springfield Township - on Springfield Pike (RT 4)
Wyoming - Springfield Township - on Springfield Pike (RT 4) - established 1869 - incorporated 1874
Yankeetown - Delhi Township

Many more housing developments are listed in *Places Names Directory of Southwest Ohio*, 1986, by Madge R. Fitak.

Amity	English Woods	Huntcrest Acres	North Clippinger	Spring Meadows
Ancor	Fairwind Acres	Idlewild	North Hills	Stanberry Park
Arborcrest Acres	Fashion Hgts.	Jones Farm	Estates	Stratford Manor
Autumn Acres	Faxon Hills	Kenridge	N. Sagamore Heights	Summit
Barwyn Acres	Forest Hills Estates	Kenwood Hills	Norwood Heights	Sunair
Beech-Mar	Fox Acres	Kenwood Knolls	Oakdale	Teakwood Acres
Beechview Estates	Foxhunter Lane	La Feuille Terrace	Paddison Hills	Turpin Hills
Britney Acres	Frontier Park	Lawyerdale Estates	Pines, The	Wardwood Acres
Brookhill	Galaxy Acres	Lynnview	Placid Meadows	Watch Farm Acres
Brookwood	Gieringer	Marlain Acres	Plantation Acres	Watch Hill
Chesswood Acres	Greenfield Village	Miami Grove	Pleasant Hills	White Oak Meadows
Compton Park	Harewood Acres	Miami Heights	Raider's Run	Whitetree
Compton Woods	Hatwell	Miami Station	Rendcomb Junction	Wildbrook Acres
Cotillion Village	High Point	Montgomery Hgts.	Riverview Hgts.	Wyoming Meadows
Country Club Acres	Hill Top Acres	Mt. Airy Center	Rolling Knolls Estates	
Cyclorama Hgts.	Holiday Acres	Mt. Washington Hgts.	Sherwood Village	
Eileen Gardens	Hollywood Estates	Mountview	South Clippinger	

Two useful websites name the towns, villages, neighborhoods, and townships of Hamilton County.

https://ohio.hometownlocator.com/counties/cities,cfips,061,c,hamilton.cfm
This site has information for 268 cities, towns, and other populated places, including links to some current maps.

https://en.wikipedia.org/wiki/List_of_Cincinnati_neighborhoods
This site has links to 1869 Titus maps for many neighborhoods.

Cincinnati, 1815

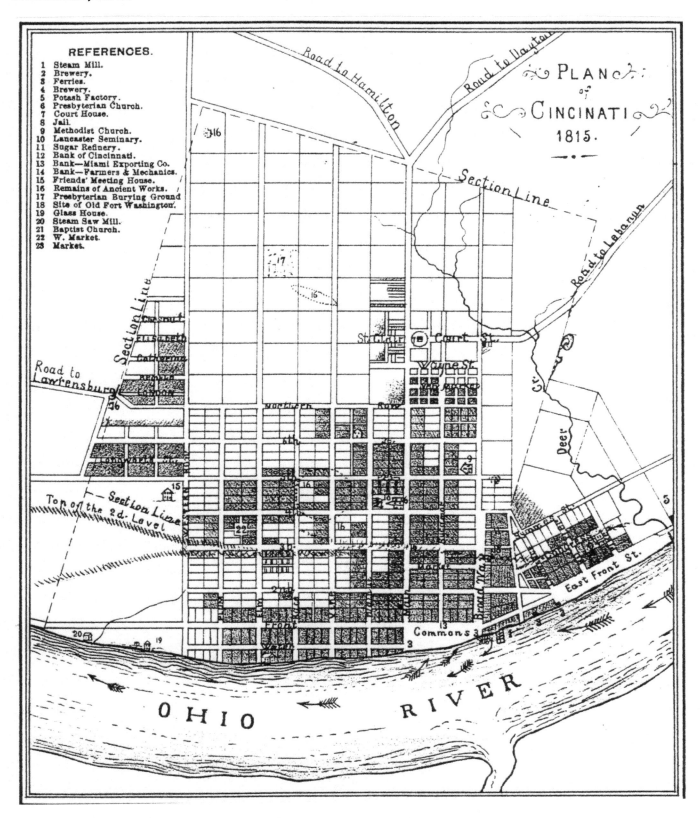

Cincinnati, 1819

https://libraries.uc.edu/arb/collections/urban-studies/cincinnati-maps.html

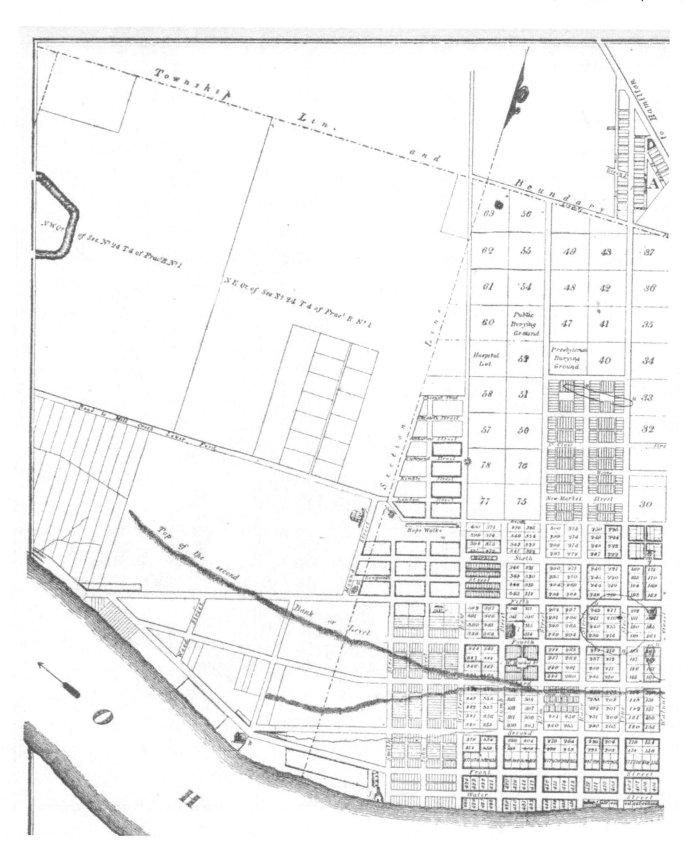

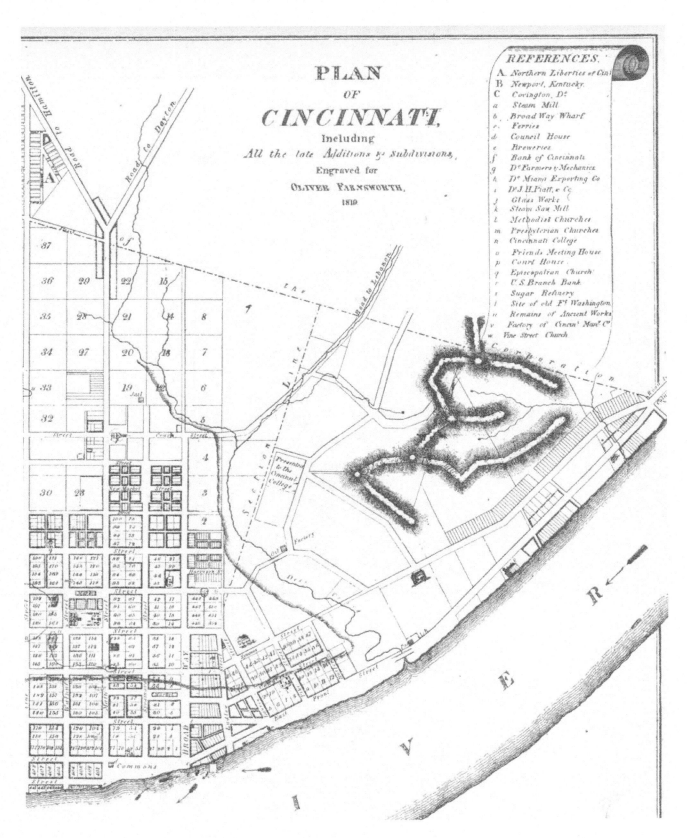

Cincinnati, 1842

https://libraries.uc.edu/arb/collections/urban-studies/cincinnati-maps.html

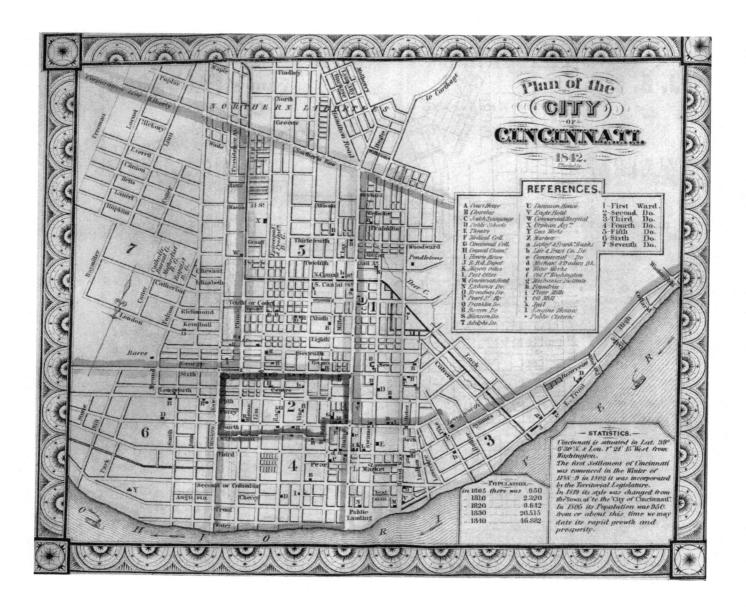

References

A. Courthouse	I. Revere House	Q. Franklin Hotel	Y. Gas Works	g. Mechanics Institute
B. Churches	J. Railroad Depot	R. Boston Hotel	Z. Markets	h. Foundries
C. Jewish Synagogue	K. Mayor's House	S. Mansion Hotel	a. Lafay & Franklin Banks	i. Flour Mills
D. Public Schools	L. Post Office	T. Adelphi Hotel	b. Life & Trust Co. Banks	j. Oil Mill
E. Theatre	M. Cincinnati Hotel	U. Dennison House	c. Commercial Bank	k. Jail
F. Medical College	N. Exchange Hotel	V. Eagle Hotel	d. Merchant & Traders Bank	l. Engine Houses
G. Cincinnati College	O. Broadway Hotel	W. Commercial Hosp	e. Water Works	o Public Cisterns
H. Council Chambers	P. Pearl St. Hotel	X. Orphan Asylum	f. Old Fort Washington	

Cincinnati, 1860

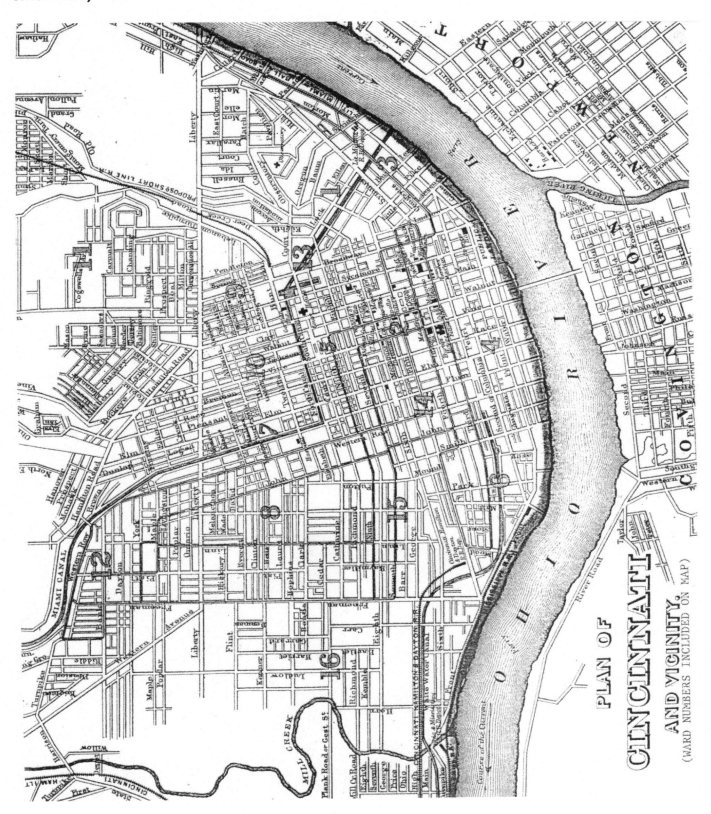

Cincinnati, 1891

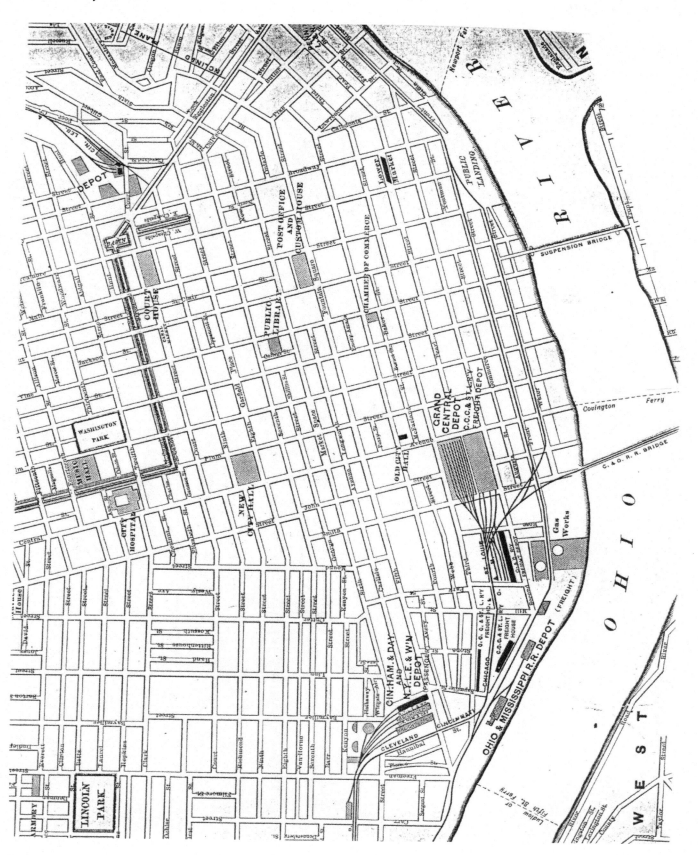

Cincinnati, 1929   https://libraries.uc.edu/arb/collections/urban-studies/cincinnati-maps.html

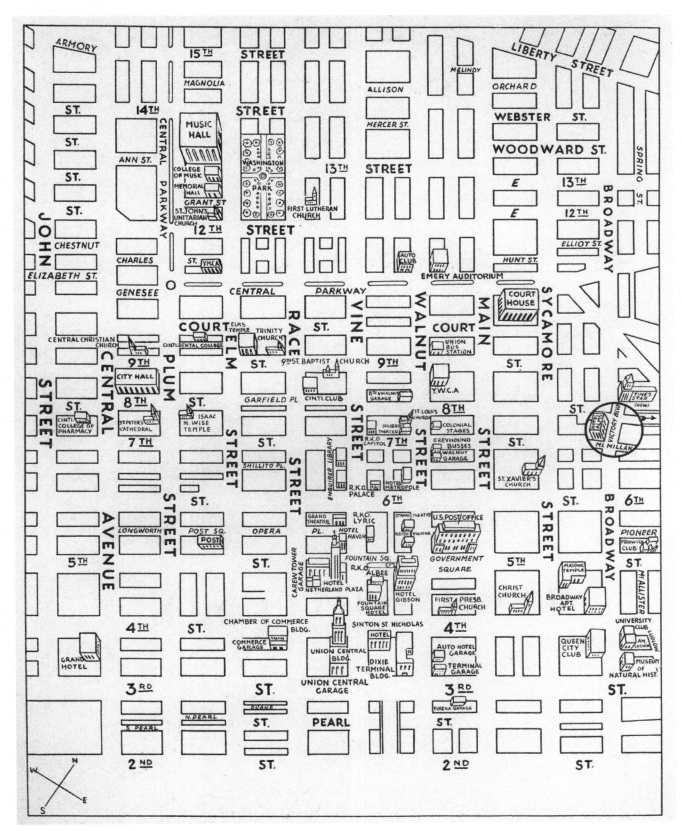

Hamilton County, 1876: Whitewater and Miami Townships

Hamilton County, 1876: Green and Delhi Townships

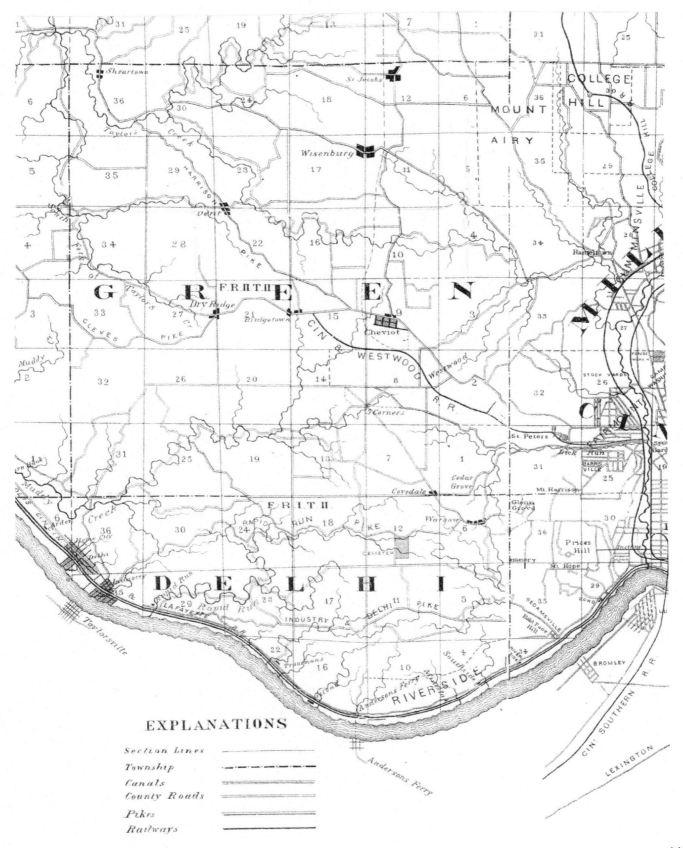

EXPLANATIONS

Section Lines
Township
Canals
County Roads
Pikes
Railways

Hamilton County, 1876: Mill Creek and Cincinnati Townships

Hamilton County, 1876: Columbia, Spencer, and Anderson Townships

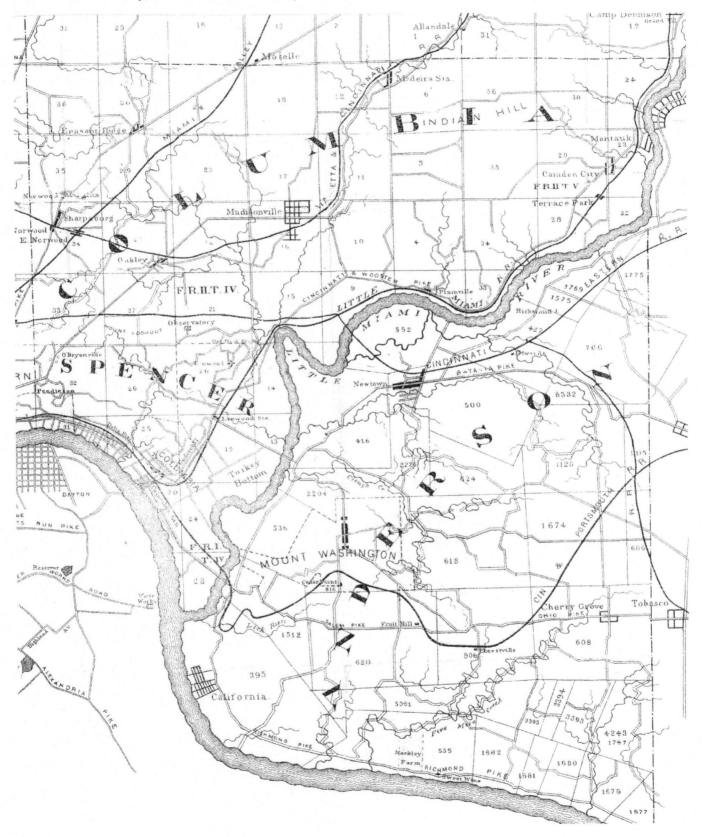

Hamilton County, 1876: Harrison, Crosby, and Whitewater Townships

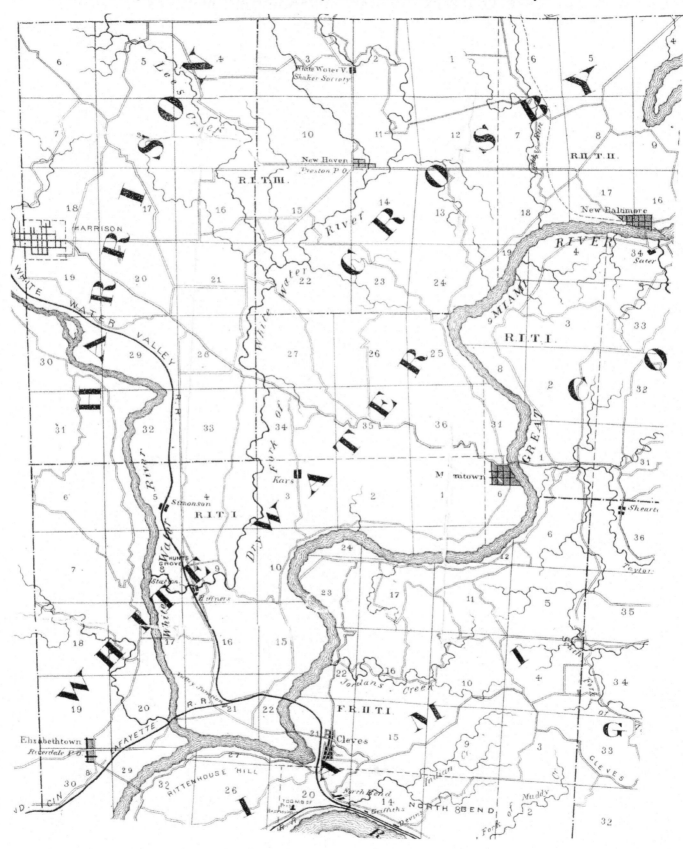

Hamilton County, 1876: Crosby and Colerain Townships

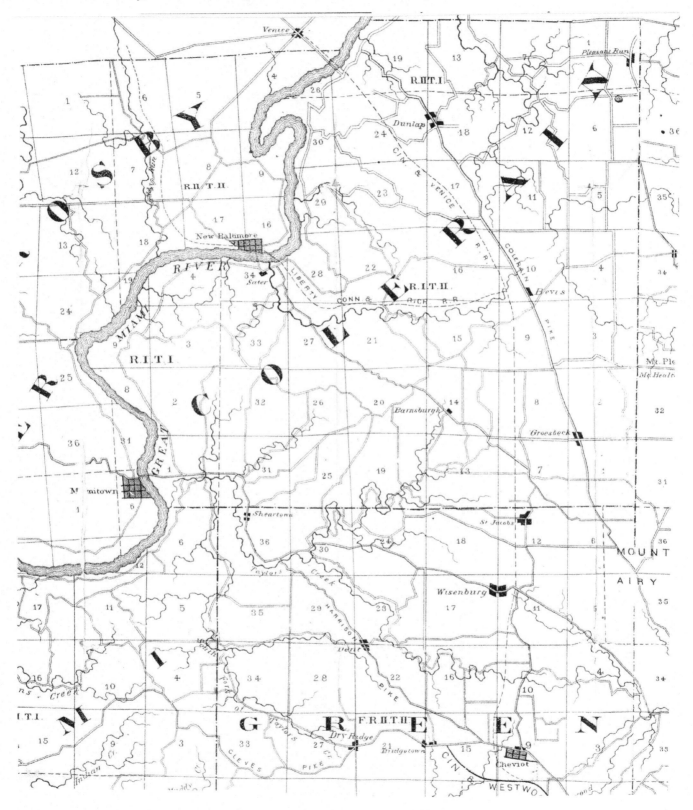

Hamilton County, 1876: Springfield and West Sycamore Townships

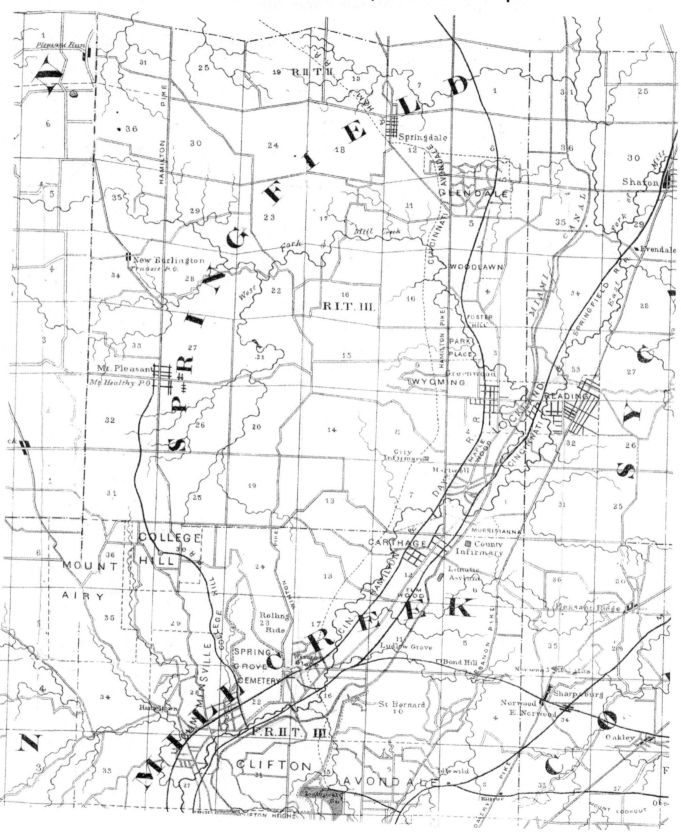

Hamilton County, 1876: East Sycamore and Symmes Townships

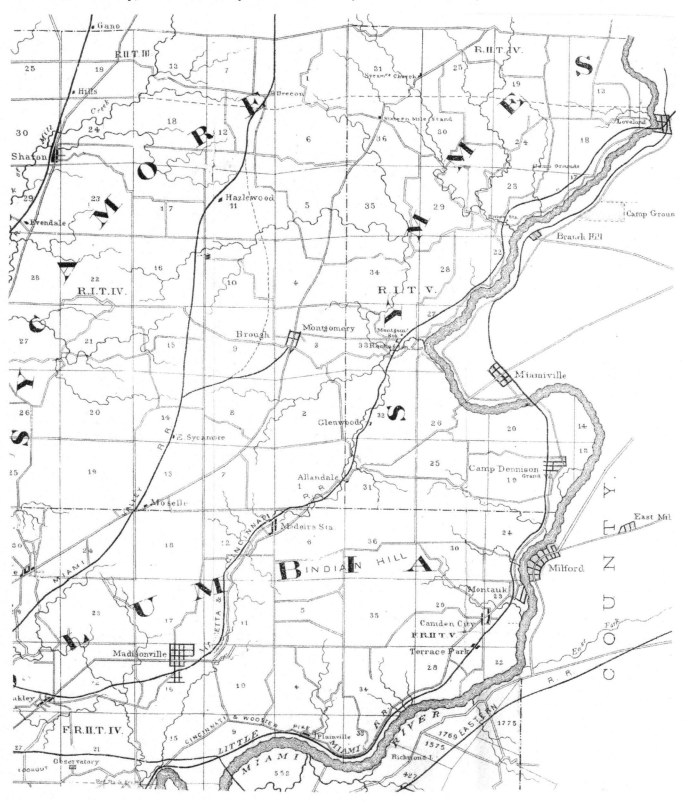

Selected Topic Index

Made in the USA
Monee, IL
24 November 2019

17368297R10072